MW00874136

The Introvert's Guide to Mastering Communication

7 Effective Techniques to Unlock the Secrets of Small Talk, Active Listening, and Social Confidence

T.J. Odinson

Contents

contained within this document, including, but not limited to, errors, omissions, or inaccuracies.

Introduction

Being introverted is not the same as being shy. Introversion is a personality type, whereas shyness is an emotion; however, the line between being an introvert and an extrovert is blurrier than most people think. Avoiding social situations because of anxiety or low self-esteem is natural, but by over-coming insecurities, this can be changed. Introverts can sometimes find it difficult to attract a romantic partner; nonetheless, this can be changed by becoming better conversationalists. The workplace is intimidating for some introverts, who may feel over-looked and appear inexperienced in confident communication.

We can all agree that conversation plays a massive part in communication; without it, there would be chaos. Whether you are an introvert, an extrovert, or someone in between, conversation is essential to daily function. The problem is that not everyone enjoys social, personal, or even professional discussions. I was in that boat not so long ago. Awkward silences were my greatest fear, which was accompanied by terrible social anxiety. My introversion was obvious, and my reservations were clearly visible. Small talk was my enemy, and fading into the background was my constant wish. Yet still, I overcame all of these things to succeed in being an introvert, living in an extroverted world. You can do the same; I am here to make that happen.

First, we will look at what confidence is, and what characteristics make up self-confidence as a whole. Confidence can be built from the inside out, while social anxiety can be controlled through the development of confidence. In that regard, you will come across some exercises such as muscle relaxation, and preparation for potential social anxiety inducing situations. Chapter 1 ends off with an explanation of charisma—and the characteristics thereof—in addition to a breakdown of other essential skills that can be used to breed confidence.

Chapter 2 begins with the notion that good conversation requires good listening skills. A distinction is drawn between hearing and listening, before active listening is examined in its different forms, one of which being listening with empathy. Patience and trustworthiness are important virtues to have when entering into conversations. Combine them with self-control and you add in a further contributor to discussions free of social anxiety or fear.

Trust is an interesting topic that I explore before moving on to look at self-control. The former is a requirement of successful relationships across the board, and the latter can be worked on to become a more patient, empathetic, and communicative person. This leads me to body language, which is the silent component of communication and impacts us consciously and subconsciously. I will introduce you to Mehrabian's theory of communication, including some interesting facts and outcomes of scientific studies. As you progress through Chapter 3, you will learn how intricate body language can be, but also how simple it can be. You will become equipped to read body language as well as how to display it in a more positive manner. Keep in mind that there are certain gestures and expressions that can be faked as well as others that are completely instinctual and unavoidable.

Sometimes, we feel the need to pacify a situation

to make ourselves feel more comfortable. Well, there is quite a bit of science involved, which you can look forward to finding out about. I will make sure to give you an understanding of the language of touch (known as haptics), including the changes in voice tone and pitch, known as paralanguage. There is a detailed section on mirroring, which explains how we mirror the actions of others, both naturally, and in a planned manner.

Following the "non-spoken communication" section, you learn more about small talk and the science behind it. Moreover, questions you may have about why we make small talk, how it is made, and what to avoid, will be answered. I will show you how to become better at small talk by highlighting the right and wrong ways to approach it. Then, I conclude Chapter 4 with an examination of ways to direct the conversation to something bigger, deeper, and more meaningful.

Chapter 5 is all about asking questions, which is important in any conversation. If one person just talks and you can't get a word in, you are in for a boring chat. You do not have to talk much, but you need the chance to ask different types of questions. I will teach you more about the importance of asking questions and take you through the good ones and the bad ones. Responses also contribute to a productive chat; therefore, you will discover the best techniques for answering questions. Additionally, something to look forward to are the ten interesting facts about talking that can be used to alleviate awkward silences or add to already-flowing conversations.

The next chapter gives you some useful acronyms such as SBR: Specific, Broad, and Related. When you are stuck for conversational material, you can call on the acronym to jog your memory on discussion techniques. There are several of them that you will learn in due course. Making and receiving compliments is covered, and there is a specific focus on how there is room for awkwardness, but also how to avoid it. Among a few other things, I will show you how to say no in a positive way, as well as how to exit a conversation without being rude. On the back of exit strategies, you will learn the art of good storytelling, and the science behind it... yes, there is actual science that explains how great storytellers evoke chemical release in the brain. In addition, I intend to reveal a set of techniques for delivery, and a breakdown of the elements that make up a good story.

The final chapter rounds everything up as I give you an extensive set of tips based on different situations. There is a focus on formal networking, such as organized networking events, and informal networking such as out-of-work casual events.

Nobody likes rejection; however, it is inevitable. Therefore, it's necessary to look at some tactics and figurative conversational counter punches. This is a very useful section, which deviates to address awkward situations that we have all been in. With a little bit of application, I am hoping to help you avoid, or minimize awkwardness.

At this stage, you may be wondering why I haven't mentioned a particular anxiety inducing situation that a lot of people would like to improve at: dating. There is a lovely section to look forward to, after which you should have some new skills for the first, second, third, or more dates.

So, get ready to step further down the path of mastering communication with an open mind and an open heart.

Chapter 1

Unlocking Your Inner Charisma

To be charismatic is to be colorful, but considering that 66% of women prefer men in black, perhaps this is not the case. Black is associated with confidence, intelligence, and sexuality, while blue is associated with dependability and stability (Smith, 2022). I guess it depends on how you dress, but there is much more to confidence than a black dress or a pair of blue jeans.

Confidence is not a fixed attribute that some have, and others don't; it is the outcome of our thoughts and actions. Confidence is not based on your ability to do something, but rather on the belief that you can do it. Let's take golf for instance, there are a plethora of players that have the same ability, but only a few make it into the pro ranks, a handful of which will experience victory. Yes, hard work is a consideration, but hard work and ability without confidence, or belief, is most often not enough.

It is a spectrum. As a scenario, picture that you have a hammer with a large head and a small nail that has to be knocked 95% of the way into a plank of wood. You would be pretty confident that you could easily get that nail fully into the plank using the hammer. This isn't a difficult task, which means you believe you can pull it off—a scenario where it is easy to be confident.

Picture another scenario; you go on a yacht trip, and the captain gets too ill to operate the yacht. You don't know how to control it, so your belief in your ability to take over is little to none. Basically, your confidence levels, in relation to operating the yacht, are terribly low (and completely understandable).

Confidence is not always a good thing. Confidently believing that you can operate the yacht doesn't mean your ability is any better than in the above scenario. Your *belief* is what brings confidence. These are obviously not examples relative to social confidence, but they explain the mechanics of confidence quite well. However, there are several qualities that are closely related to confidence, and I would just like to say that we must not conflate confidence with arrogance.

Self-Esteem

Self-esteem is highly subjective because it only considers what you think of yourself. If you don't like how you look, conclude that others don't find you interesting, or believe that you are no good at anything, then you will have low self-esteem. Consequently, your confidence will align with your self-esteem. So, if you are not confident in yourself, then confidence in a social setting is highly unlikely.

Optimism

We all know the "glass half full" adage; well, that is optimism put into a sentence. In essence, being optimistic is to expect the best, or at the least, a good outcome of a situation. Real confidence, not faked or put-on confidence, harnesses optimism. If you are pessimistic and foresee the worst outcome, real confidence is always absent.

Self-Compassion

Being compassionate means being kind and under-standing. When we apply that to our own disposition and actions, we display self-compassion. It is about *not* castigating ourselves for a failure or an inade-quacy. The effect on confidence is that failure is soft-ened because we understand that failures happen. This makes it easier to be confident on the basis that if we don't try, we won't know... so we might as well try.

Self-Efficacy

Belief that you can succeed at a task embodies self-efficacy, which is extremely similar to confidence. The theory is that with each task that you complete, your self-efficacy (and confidence) grows.

Why Is Self-Confidence Important?

The simple answer is that being self-confident improves your life. Studies show that it is associated with better health and have gone as far to conclude that high self-confidence increases chances of surviving a serious medical procedure (Mann, et al., 2004)

Data from several research papers indicates that individuals with high self-esteem, and thus high confidence, enjoy a greater sense of self-worth (Stankov, 2013).

Furthermore, data from scientific studies indicate greater life enjoyment, absence of self-doubt, more enjoyable social interactions, and elevated levels of energy (Sinusoid, 2021).

As previously mentioned, confidence is present in most people, so let's look at how it can be stoked into action if it is not prominent enough.

Building Inner Confidence

You are not just going to snap your fingers and suddenly have high self-confidence. There is work that needs to be put in. For that reason, I would recommend a systematic approach, starting at point A and building from there.

The Root Cause

To rectify lack of confidence, you need to pinpoint the actual problem. This task should be undertaken in a way in which you do not judge yourself for your perceived negative traits or inadequacies. Remember that you are building your self-confidence, and that judgment is not going to help. Here are four exercises that you can do to help you identify the source of your low self-confidence and how to resolve it.

1. Carry a notebook and jot down any persistent thoughts that affect your confidence.
2. Identify the source of those thoughts— perhaps you view yourself in a poor light because of a childhood experience that has stuck around or from exiting a toxic romantic relationship. Asking the "who, why, and what" questions will be useful to narrow down the source.
3. Make a conscious effort to eradicate the thoughts. This is a difficult task because some of these thoughts may have been with you for many years.
4. Create a plan from the "now" going forward. The human brain favors the negative, so your low self-confidence creating thoughts are easier to think than positive ones. It is almost as if you need to retrain your brain to build optimism.

Self-Confidence for You

Everyone is different, and the meaning of confidence differs from person to person. Let's assume that your current confidence stumbling block is a conversation that you want to have with your boss. He or she made you feel uncomfortable by sharing the contents of a confidential discussion, and you are struggling to confront them. You know what you want to do, and you know that it is the right thing to do, so for you personally, your confidence will be having that important discussion. It may not be something as specific as that. Perhaps, you are generally low in confidence when it comes to discussions with the opposite sex. In this case, your personal confidence would be initiating a conversation and feeling comfortable while the discussion takes place. When you know what confidence is in your personal context, you have taken the first step toward achieving your desired level of confidence.

Align With Yourself

Most of us are guilty of telling ourselves that we should have done things differently or should be in a specific position in life at the age that we are. These thoughts often stem from comparing ourselves with others or imposing what society generally accepts.

You need to decide what *you* want and stop using the word "should." Aligning with yourself leads to making more confident decisions.

Small Steps

If you try to change or improve on ten things at once, you will probably become overwhelmed and end up not improving on any of them. The same goes for addressing and heightening your confidence... little by little.

The Growth Mindset

Remaining for improvement is a mindset that promotes growth as a person because it doesn't impose limitations. See it as a journey. You haven't reached the end... yet. Your confidence isn't where it should be... yet. This particular task is difficult, and I don't know how to do it... yet. You get what I'm saying.

Failure Happens, and That's Okay

Every single great achiever in this world has failed on numerous occasions. It is completely normal, and you need to accept that. For example, you may ask someone out on a date, and it turns out to be a disaster. So what? There are way more people that you will be incompatible with than compatible with. The date didn't go as planned, but you can't let it dent your confidence or perpetuate ideas that you are not interesting or not fun to be around.

Stand Up to Yourself

That voice in your head is not necessarily correct, so when you find your inner voice being critical and telling you that you are not good enough, you have to take the power back and assert that you are good enough. You are probably your harshest critic, as most of us are, but we can change that. Writing down assertions that go against your inner voice, will help you to monitor your mindset change.

The Temporary Nature of Emotions and Feelings

The adage about facing your fear comes to mind. The fear is temporary, and when faced, is no longer prevalent. Understand that whatever is holding you back and limiting your confidence is temporary and will come to an end. A bit of action is required, but you can get past a feeling or emotion and release your confidence.

Control What You Can

A trip to the beach may be spoiled by rain, and while that is disappointing, you can't get too upset because it is something you have zero control over. Answering questions well in a job interview and putting your best self across are things that you can control to a large degree. This is where your confidence comes from, but don't let the possibility of a question on which you have no knowledge lower your confidence level. When analyzing a situation after it has happened, pay attention to the things that you were able to control and praise yourself for doing so. That self-praise, as long as it is justified, on a continuous basis, has great effects on growing one's confidence.

Like-Mindedness

When actively working on your confidence, you can use outside factors like podcasts, blogs, or therapists that all have the thread of improved confidence running through them. Also, you should be spending time with people that build you up, and that are good for your confidence. That is why we seek out like-minded people as friends and partners.

Compassion

Forgive yourself for mistakes, embarrassing occasions, or failures. Holding onto past happenings doesn't achieve anything. Be kind to yourself and move forward where possible. We should all strive to be compassionate to others, as well as to ourselves.

Overcoming Social Anxiety

Social anxiety is characterized by a fear of social interactions, often stemming from low self-confidence. We do not want to be judged and are scared of saying the wrong things, which is very limiting in "normal" social conversations. We often avoid putting ourselves in those situations, but sometimes we have no choice. In such cases, it can be physically and emotionally uncomfortable. We get sweaty palms, feel nervous, and have an increased heartbeat, among other limiting factors that ensure we can't relax and enjoy social situations. The following is a list of additional symptoms and signs that you may experience if you are socially anxious:

- Worry about everyday events such as going shopping, having work conversations, or having to make small talk with strangers.
- Avoid group conversations, birthday dinners, or general gatherings.
- Worry that you will do something to embarrass yourself in a social setting.

- Feel like other people are judging you, criticizing you, or talking badly about you.

There are a range of techniques that you can use to manage and overcome social anxiety. The most confident people in this world encounter moments of social anxiety. Although it will never go away, controlling what you can will allow you to reduce your anxiety considerably.

Controlled Breathing

Controlled breathing exercises are useful if you feel anxious about something socially related. We all know how to do this - big breath in through the nose, hold, release slowly through the mouth. Try to focus very closely on the feeling of the air entering your lungs, the way your chest rises, and the air exiting your lungs as you exhale. This is a partial relaxation technique, but the close focus is also intended as a distraction from your feelings of anxiety.

Muscle Relaxation

Tense up all your muscles, hold for a few seconds, and release. Similarly, to the breathing exercise, focus on how your muscles feel during tension and release. Walking or jogging, and other forms of physical exertion before or after muscle relaxation on a semi-regular basis can help with overall anxiety.

Preparation

If you play a sport, then you have to prepare for every game by practicing. You can also prepare for potential anxiety-inducing social situations. As silly as it sounds, doing a role-play exercise that mimics something that fuels your anxiety with a friend or family member is a great way to prepare for the real thing. If you are prepared, your confidence should be up in any case.

Change Focus

Instead of thinking that you are being judged and that everyone is going to be privately critical of you, focus on the conversation at hand. You may find that things are not as awkward as you had imagined. Chances are that the people around you can't tell that you are anxious, and as the discussion continues, your anxiety is quite likely to ease or dissipate completely. Back yourself!

Reframing Negativity

Instead of saying or thinking that a situation will make you too anxious to deal with, you can reframe that by saying or thinking that you have felt anxious in situations before and have always gotten through them. It is not quite a mind trick, but it is a quickfire way of putting a positive spin on something.

General

Even if you have social anxiety, you may know very little about what it is. Do some reading and research. I would recommend the WebMD site as a good starting point. The more you know about your anxiety, the easier it is to address it. Seeking therapy can be an excellent route. If you have a good therapist, they will have lots of management techniques, and having the science explained to you can be liberating.

The Mystery of Charisma

Charisma is something that is easier to spot than to describe. Nonetheless, a 2018 study into characteristics of charisma narrowed it down to affability and influence (Tskhay et al., 2018). The study, published in the *Journal of Personality and Social Psychology*, defined affability as being emotionally approachable and influence as a magnetism that attracts attention. It was concluded that people who are charismatic generally display warmth and a sense of competence, with strong social communication skills, both verbal and nonverbal. Charismatic individuals are likable and tend to be unconventional to a small degree, which is perhaps a trait that garners likeability.

Charisma is often divided into three broad categories, which then have further sub-categories. Let's take a look.

Being Present

These days, we are dependent on our electronic devices, highly distractible and struggle to be present while focusing only on the thing that we are doing at the time. If you are on a date with someone and they keep checking their phone, you will probably feel like they don't value you as important. However, if you are being given that person's full attention, you will feel like they value your time together. In order to be present, you need to do the following:

1. Bring yourself back to the here and now. If you are engaging in a conversation and your mind starts thinking of your latest Instagram post, catch yourself, and refocus on the present.
2. Make sure you are comfortable.
3. Leave your phone in the car, or turn it off... not just on silent: *off*.
4. Look the person in the eye.
5. Nod to show that you are listening and

ask intermittent questions if clarification is required.

6. Avoid fidgeting. Some people are more fidgety than others, but it gives the impression that you are not interested and thus not present.

7. Don't start planning the response in your head. Allow the other person to finish, and wait a few seconds before you talk.

Holding the Power

In her book, *The Charisma Myth,* Olivia Fox Cabane states the following about power in the context of charisma:

Power means being perceived as able to affect the world around us, whether through influence on or authority over others, large amounts of money, expertise, intelligence, sheer physical strength, or high social status.

This definition is both wide and specific, but the important part is that of influence and to a lesser extent, authority. Power can manifest negatively, and as awful as it is to say, many dictators and warlords are charismatic leaders. We are talking about the good kind of charisma. Therefore, the power element can be achieved by:

1. Knowing a little about a range of subjects. People who read a lot tend to have good general knowledge and can hold a conversation on a range of different subjects. If you have few limits in what you can talk about, then you will have the confidence to talk to many people.

2. Getting fit. If you are in shape, you feel better about yourself. Simple.

3. Dressing well. Much like being in shape, dressing well makes you feel good about yourself, and other people will notice. Even wearing something slightly off-beat or unusual can be a sign of charisma.

4. Occupying the space. You may likely fade into the background if you sit with your hands on your lap or hunched over. You should rather sit up straight, shoulders back, and be a presence.

5. Take control. If you sit down at a restaurant and move the salt shaker or the jug of water, your subconscious assumes you are in control, which means that others will sense your control.

6. Slow down your speech, so as to negate
    the impression of nervousness, but also
    to hold the floor.

Just a brief point of clarity: not everyone wants to be charismatic, so faking these things is not a good idea. You can still overcome social anxiety without being the center of attention, but at least you are gaining the knowledge to boost your charisma if you wish to do so.

Warmth

The third element is probably the most difficult to fake and is a virtue that could be said to be natural in a majority of cases. I like to compare it to singing. A good singer just sings without thinking about it, whereas a poor singer will think about their breathing and the way that they are sitting so as not to restrict lung capacity. Some people are warm, and other people have to put in the work to be warm, which is absolutely fine as long as it is genuine warmth. People that are naturally warm will do the following without thinking, but if you want to learn to be warm, you can put them into effect with some thought and focus on the following:

1. Think of yourself as the host in social

situations, with the goal of making people comfortable, as if they were attending an event at your home. The relaxation part is the fact that they are not at your home.

2. Give a firm handshake and don't break eye contact. Well, do break eye contact but not while you are shaking hands

3. Make an effort to give compliments, but make sure that they are genuine. The more charismatic amongst us will do this without faltering, and the immediacy of the compliment is evidence that it is meant as genuine.

4. Sprinkle your voice with warmth... but don't be fake. Yes, I know, similar to compliments.

5. Mirror body language. This tip has been around for decades. The thinking is that if you very subtly make the same movements as the other person a short time after they have (say, crossed their legs), you create a subconscious trust.

6. Have a relaxed posture or stance that is non-threatening.

7. Smile. That's all.

On an ongoing basis, you should make an effort to:

- Remember important dates and events.
- Be thoughtful about gifts that you give.
- Help without being asked (try to read the situation and if you are not quite certain that your help will be wanted, rather offer before diving straight in).
- Ask for help if you need it.

Can Charisma Be Learned?

This question comes back to the example of singing without thinking. You get naturals, and you get learners that need to put in the work. Singing can be learned but only to a point, and the same is the case with charisma. Faking having a good singing voice is tough and so is faking a charismatic persona. However, to answer the question in short, before expanding, yes, charisma can be learned, but a learner will never become as good as a natural.

You can still be charismatic even though you're introverted. In fact, many introverts are very charismatic, but if you really want to learn how to be charismatic, you can implement the following:

1. Display confidence, but not arrogance—
   sometimes there can be a fine line, and
   sometimes confidence can be mistaken
   for arrogance... it is an ever so slightly
   double-edged sword.
2. Be authentic.
3. Become a positive person.
4. Don't be afraid to show your
   vulnerabilities.
5. Listen attentively instead of half-
   listening because you are focusing on
   what you intend to say next.

Doing these things can indeed increase your charisma, but be mindful of the fact that there is a lot of information out there about faking charisma. I really don't want that to be a goal—if you want to be more charismatic, work towards it for the right reasons with warmth being the most important.

Other Essential Social Skills

Making a good first impression is something that we should all aim for. As humans, we are extremely judgmental, often very quickly. Therefore, in order to optimize your first impression, you need to:

- be on time
- dress appropriately for the situation
- be yourself
- smile
- use small talk
- avoid negativity
- be courteous and attentive

You also need to make an effort to remember names. For some, the name is gone even before the handshake has been concluded, but making an effort to remember the name of a casual acquaintance, will leave a great impression when you run into that person and call them by name.

Sometimes, social interactions will call for an apology, and you want to get your apology right to rescue a situation or remedy a wrong that you have committed. It is a skill to make a genuine apology and have it come across as heartfelt and authentic.

When apologizing, you have to be doing so for the right reasons. Often, we will see a celebrity issuing an apology for something that they said, and everyone knows it is just an exercise in saving face. These types of apologies don't really assume respon-sibility, but when apologizing, you need to get across that you feel responsible and also that you regret having done or said something. An offer to make amends, if possible, is recommended.

One would hope that an apology would not become confrontational. However, there are times when we need to confront someone out of concern, and we want that interaction to be as non-confrontational as possible. That does sound like a contradiction, but if you have a friend who is starting to succumb to alcoholism, the confrontation is necessary, although it needs to be handled kindly. This is probably your quintessential example of something coming from a place of compassion that could get ugly. Whatever the case, my best advice is to proceed with caution, express your concern and care, show empathy, and make sure the other person knows that you want the best for them. Confrontation is inevitable, and handling one in a positive way that produces a good outcome is a very sought-after social skill.

Have You Unlocked Your Charisma?

At the risk of repeating myself, I must end this chapter by saying that more charisma may not be your goal, but greater confidence is what you are after. The above analysis of charisma and the associated topics should have increased your under-standing of what it means to be confident. You definitely know that conversation is a massive part of social existence, and having good conversations is a skill that can do wonders for your confidence. It is time to progress as I teach you all about becoming an accomplished conversationalist.

Chapter 2

The Key to Great Conversations

"People love to talk but hate to listen. Listening is not merely not talking, though even that is beyond most of our powers; it means taking a vigorous, human interest in what is being told to us. You can listen like a blank wall or like a splendid auditorium where every sound comes back fuller and richer." –Alice Duer Miller

The American writer, Alice Duer Miller, who died in 1942, had quite an impact on the literary world, as a contributor to the feminist movement. Miller had a thing or two to say about listening too, and the quote above is a great way to kick off this chapter.

Why Is Listening Important?

Nowadays, we all have access to GPS, but when we had to stop and ask for directions, listening was an essential requirement. Although this is a very colloquial example, it is one that makes complete sense. We need to listen to make any progress, be it in the form of progression in a conversation or otherwise. Here are some of the things that make listening important:

- it allows people to build trust
- it reduces misunderstandings and eliminates conflict
- it encourages empathy
- it can improve relationships and deepen friendships
- it can increase leadership and productivity

Hearing Versus Listening

The saying, "In through one ear and out the other" could be used to loosely create the distinction between listening and hearing. If there is something else on your mind, you may hear someone speaking and understand the words but forget very quickly thereafter, perhaps intentionally. We hear sounds on a daily basis, whether we want to or not. This type of hearing is involuntary and completely passive (such as hearing a hooter or your neighbor coughing), whereas listening during a conversation should be intentional, voluntary, and active.

To carry out a productive conversation, all parties need to listen to what the others are saying. It seems obvious, but I'm sure you have been in one-sided conversations where another participant is not interested and gives the bare minimum. I would say that most of us have been on both sides of the fence, i.e., being a genuine participant and being a reluctant participant. The reasons may differ, but the ability to hold a *good* conversation is a trait of a confident person.

Active Listening

Formulating good, confident conversation, can be assisted by active listening—a great skill to have. It is not particularly difficult to learn and is largely based on clarifying what has been said. A common human trait is not asking questions because we do not want to sound stupid. For an introvert, or socially awkward individual, this trait can be particularly prominent because there is already that underlying fear of being judged. Try to remember that asking questions during a conversation is a good thing that conveys interest and the desire to completely understand.

Being fully present and making eye contact during discussions are the first two elements, but you need to be aware of non-verbal cues as well. Open and non-threatening body language will go a long way in establishing and maintaining a safe space. After the conversation has started, there will be times when you need to ask questions. Open-ended questions are best because they call for more than just a yes-or-no answer. For example:

- That sounds like a very interesting experience, could you please tell me a bit more about it?
- I get what you are saying, but how do you personally feel about it?
- The mention of "personal" reflects the warmth that we dealt with earlier.
- Sorry, I don't quite understand. Is this what you mean? (Say what you think it means).

- I'm not sure what I would have done in that situation. What do you think?

The above are very nondescript but can be applied to any circumstance, with a bit of variation. Basically, you are trying to make the other person or people comfortable while ensuring that you understand what is being said.

Another technique is reflection; where you summarize what you have heard and ask if you heard it correctly. You can use introductory phrases like, "in other words..." or "so you mean...". Using this technique can also weed out the irrelevant or insignificant parts of what has been said, like a day of the week, or the weather, unless such detail meaningfully contributes to what is being spoken of.

Being patient makes for a better conversation, as it limits interruptions. Having said that, a well-timed interruption to get clarity is fine. You could say something like, "I'm sorry to interrupt, but I just need to be clear on X, Y, and Z." I realize that this is in contradiction to the "let them finish" maxim. However, it is justified in circumstances where you become confused or struggle to follow the line of discussion.

In a conversation, it is easy to jump to conclusions or make judgments on another person's opinions. There is no issue with hearing an opinion, disagreeing, and politely conveying your disagreement. If you mix in judgment, then you are likely to alienate other participants and perhaps alienate yourself too.

Active listening is often referred to as having three A's.

Attention

A 1957 book entitled, *Listening is a 10-Part Skill* set out the following listening facts, mixed with a valid opinion (Nichols, 1957):

A typical person can speak 125 words-per-minute, yet we can process up to three times faster, reaching as much as 500 words-per-minute. The poor listener grows impatient, while the effective listener uses the extra processing time to process the speaker's words, distinguish key points, and mentally summarize them.

The author, Ralph G. Nichols is saying that instead of mentally willing the other participant in the conversation to finish their point, we should take in every detail and make use of the extra time to pay full attention to what is being said.

Attitude

If you enter into a discussion with thoughts that it will be a waste of time, you are not committed to the discussion and have already written off its productivity with your negative attitude. Introversion can be accompanied by this type of attitude, but it doesn't *always* come from a bad place. Sometimes, the negative attitude is because of social anxiety and has nothing to do with the actual person or conversation. How often have you dreaded spending time with someone or going to a movie that you think you won't like but end up having fun or enjoying the experience? I would venture to say this happens quite often. So, if you can focus on the good outcome or possible good outcome of a discussion, you are going in with an open-minded attitude—the right kind!

Adjustment

The third 'A' is regularly interpreted as an adjustment to the way in which you listen, which is not to say is incorrect. But adjustment also refers to adjusting your views and opinions based on what you hear during a conversation. Changing the way that you listen may involve adjusted mannerisms, less clarity seeking, and more nodding, for instance. In addition, it may involve adjusting your stance on a controversial issue when presented with evidence or an opinion that holds more weight than your own.

Benefits of Active Listening

Active listening has many benefits, and I would venture to say that it doesn't have disadvantages, unless you conflate clarifying questions with constant interruptions, and so on. Active listening conveys empathy, and empathy is valuable in building meaningful relationships. In addition to the above, active listening is good for emotional management and learning not to react instantaneously based on the first emotion that you feel. You will be able to retain more information through active listening, which allows for better conflict-resolution and problem-solving. In a healthy discussion involving mutual active listening, the parties involved will feel validated, and their opinions valued.

If you are thinking that things are getting a bit too technical and all you are after is a conversation at a dinner party that is void of awkwardness, I completely understand. In light thereof, and before we move on, here is a point-form summary (with additions) of ways to improve your active-listening skills:

- paraphrase
- ask specific questions
- make your questions open-ended
- use affirmations
- nod, smile, and maintain eye contact
- be patient
- disclose similar situations that you have faced
- take a genuine interest
- get rid of distractions
- empathize
- withhold judgment

If you are likely to have or want to have more conversations with someone, then it is a good idea to find out more about things that they mention. It is flattering if someone starts to tell you about their hobby and you do a bit of Googling, so you have a bit more knowledge.

Soon enough, these active-listening techniques will become completely natural. It is like muscle memory. If you swing a golf club enough times, you will not even think about what you are doing: it becomes natural. Same, same with active listening.

Empathetic Listening

The word empathy has cropped up a few times, but I haven't officially defined it. The Merriam-Webster definition is as follows:

The action of understanding, being aware of, being sensitive to, and vicariously experiencing the feelings, thoughts, and experience of another of either the past or present without having the feelings, thoughts, and experience fully communicated objectively.

To summarize, empathy is understanding another's feelings (from experience). In order to do so, we need to listen. Empathetic listening is important because, without it, our emotional connections are stifled or not even made. We should want to show care and concern, plus create an environment where empathy flows both ways.

You can put empathy into action slowly and surely in your daily life. It is generally accepted that our ability to empathize remains the same. However, as I mentioned earlier, ability is not enough. Action is required to fulfill the ability, and here are a few ways to start:

1. Develop curiosity

2. A lot of people are automatically curious and interested in what makes others tick. You can develop your curiosity by asking more questions in conversations. It is a case of inviting another person to open up to you, and most often, if your sincerity is evident, then people will open up.

3. Talking to strangers in random situations, like when in a long queue or at a sports fixture or concert, is a great way to develop your curiosity. Remember that the two latter examples have a good chance of carrying like-mindedness because the enjoyment of sport or music is mutual.

4. Focus on similarities

5. Imagine if your biggest interest was dinosaurs. You would find it easier to engage in discussions about dinosaurs and would appreciate someone who has similar interests.

6. We can be hesitant about differences and tend to see differences as a bad thing. Putting that aside opens doors to more productive conversations.

7. Listen and share

8. Imagine if a person opened up to you about a childhood experience that was particularly distressing. They are showing their vulnerability, and non-judgmental listening, plus sharing something that exposes your vulnerabilities, is a clear breeder of empathy.

Empathy creates trust and understanding, which is why it is a relationship builder and strengthener. Just like active listening, there are ways to phrase sentences when listening with empathy (this is, of course, also active listening). For example:

- Thank you for sharing that information. It must have been difficult for you.
- I can relate to what you are going through.
- It may be easier to give up, but please keep going, and I will be here for you.
- You are doing the best you can. Always remember that.
- How did you feel when that happened?
- Would you like to tell me more?

- This question is open-ended and not forceful—this is very important.
- What would be the best way forward if you had to choose one?
- Can I help in any way? Only if you want me to do so, of course.

There are many approaches to realizing the potential of your empathy. Here is a quickfire list of some that we haven't dealt with yet:

- Use your imagination to put yourself in someone else's shoes.
- Allow the other person to have a good, old rant and get everything out. We all need to do this from time to time.
- Focus on both the facts and the associated feelings.
- Provide encouragement.
- Build the person up if they are speaking negatively about themselves.

As you work on your empathetic listening, it will get better, but before we get to sympathy as a comparison to empathy, it is important to distinguish between the two types of empathy.

Emotional Empathy

Feeling the same feeling as another person is emotional empathy. Real compassion and being upset, as if you are in someone else's situation, also qualifies. This isn't something that can be forced, but it is admirable if you can reach this level of empathy. It shows that you truly care, and that is never a bad thing.

Cognitive Empathy

As the name suggests, using our cognition to understand another person's position is cognitive empathy. It is not necessarily experiencing the same feelings but having a grasp of those feelings from your own experiences.

Empathy Versus Sympathy

We know by now what empathy is, so let's focus on sympathy. Feeling sorry for someone without putting yourself in their situation and expressing that is sympathy. Judgment can accompany sympathy. For instance, someone that you work with makes a serious mistake and is issued a written warning. You can put your arm around that person and tell them that you're sorry about the written warning while still judging them (silently) for their mistake.

We shouldn't judge, but I am making sympathy sound like it lacks authenticity. This is not always the case, but the distinction is that with empathy, you feel the other person's pain, and with sympathy, you comfort the other person without taking on their pain.

I'm reluctant to offer an opinion on whether empathy is better than sympathy or vice versa because it is situation dependent. However, I think it is important to look at a few virtues that could transform sympathy into empathy.

Patience

Fundamentally, patience is the ability to wait; however, suppressing impatience in a scenario where you are forced to wait doesn't mean that you have patience. Remaining calm is the real measure of patience, but there are three different manifestations of *calm,* as patience (Schnitker, 2012). Interpersonal patience refers to being patient with other people, in relationships, at work, and in interactions with young children. Life-hardship patience is perseverance after a major setback in life, and daily hassle patience is the ability to remain calm through everyday annoyances.

Having a conversation with an impatient person isn't much fun, so here are some tips on how to become more patient:

- Get to the root cause of what it is that makes you impatient and resolve not to let it do so. (You're thinking "impossible" —it's not. It just requires some work).
- When you start to feel impatient, think of the kindest person you know, and act as they would.
- You become uncomfortable in situations where you have to wait. Accept that feeling, but try to change it.
- Instead of rushing, which we all tend to do, slow down and tell yourself that you don't have to rush.
- Try to lighten up a bit and be more relaxed generally.
- Endeavor to manage your time better.
- Make spoken or written-down assertions to be more patient on a daily basis.

Developing overall patience is not directly

related to confidence, but it should contribute to empathy, which in turn helps with better conversational outcomes, which in turn builds confidence with every conversation.

Trustworthiness

Have you ever told someone something private about yourself or something that you want to be kept confidential, only to have that person tell someone else? Of course, you have, and you have probably been guilty of the same. Breaking trust makes it very hard to fix, but displaying trustworthiness has mostly positive results. Here's how to do it:

- Be transparent about what you expect from someone else, and ask them to be transparent about their expectations of you.
- Make sure you keep in confidence what you have been requested to keep in confidence.
- Think about the consequences of your actions if you were to break trust and reverse the roles to explore what it would feel like if your trust was broken.

- Be consistent.
- Do what you believe is right, even if it makes you unpopular.
- Don't talk about how great you are.
- Help other people when they need it: this is a two-way street.
- Be honest with yourself, admit when you have made a mistake, and allow your feelings to show.

Trust takes time to build and almost no time to break. Keep that in mind when you feel the morality of your trustworthiness is being tested.

Self-Control

Imagine shouting at someone who you deem to have stolen your parking spot at the mall. That person jumps out of their car and beats you up. Had you maintained self-control, and decided it wasn't worth making a scene, you wouldn't have a black eye. I am not advocating shouting or violence, but the point is that lacking self-control often produces adverse results.

Psychologists have defined self-control as: "The ability to control behaviors to avoid temptations and achieve goals. The ability to delay gratification and resist unwanted behaviors or urges." (Duckworth et al., 2011). It is also believed that self-control is a limited resource that can be depleted.

There are three types of self-control, namely:

- Impulse Control
- If someone kicks you in the shin, your first thought is to kick them back. If someone hurls an insult your way, you are likely to hurl one straight back. These examples are of immediate and impulsive behavior.
- Emotional Control
- Overreacting to innocuous situations is an indicator of a lack of emotional control. If someone cancels plans for a valid reason, and you get very angry, you probably fall into this category.
- Movement Control
- Not really important for our purposes, but restless leg syndrome is a prime example.

A *Stress in America* survey conducted by the American Psychological Association (APA) found that 27% of respondents identified a lack of willpower as the primary factor keeping them from reaching their goals (APA, 2012).

Some examples of good self-control are as follows:

- Not using social media at work to maintain productivity.
- Not buying something you want, so you can stick to a budget.
- Cutting down on sugar intake (and sticking to it).
- Respond calmly when you are angry, upset, or frustrated.

There are ways to improve your self-control, partially by changing your circumstances, reasoning with yourself, and altering bad habits. Here are some tips on how to do it:

1. Avoid temptation. Don't put yourself in a situation where you can be tempted by food, alcohol, gambling, excessive spending, or whatever else it is that you are trying to exercise control over. If it is a verbal- or physical-fight scenario, then

walk away to avoid doing something that you will regret later.

2. Plan ahead. If you are aware of instances that may test your self-control, you probably know this from experience. Perhaps, you don't want to admit to past mistakes, but if you take something positive out of that mistake, it should be knowledge of what to do better. The next time, you can apply what you have learned with some good pre-planning.

3. Practice exercising self-control. Start in small doses, like turning down a bar of chocolate or holding off buying that new top using your credit card. These small additions will slowly add up, improving your self-control as you go.

4. One goal at a time. If you make a long list of areas in which you want to have more self-control, you may become overwhelmed and end up doing nothing. Rather, break your goals down and attack one before moving on to the next.

5. Remind yourself of the consequences. If you are trying to stop eating junk food, think of the adverse effects on your body.

Maybe you have a problem with drinking and driving. If so, then think of the possibility of crashing and hurting yourself or someone else. The idea is that thoughts of the consequences, which are usually adverse, should act as a mental deterrent from having no self-control.

6. Self-monitoring. Jot down how you are doing in the self-control department. When you see the progress that you have made in writing, it is more powerful and instills further motivation. Doing this should develop a culture of being accountable to yourself for your own actions. Don't disappoint yourself!

7. Visualize. Play out a hypothetical scenario in your mind, and try different reactions to what is going on to test which would suit the situation best.

Self-control is, of course, not a contributor to better conversations in every instance, but developing self-control puts you in a more patient atmosphere when it comes to listening. Using that patience and listening more than talking can go a long way to ease social anxiety if combined with the exercises discussed previously.

As important as listening is, we can't forget that there are other factors that allow us to communicate without talking at all. I am referring to body language and how powerful it can be in reinforcing and expanding on spoken words. Some call it the "silent conversation," and as would be appropriate on that note, the chapter on listening will close.

Chapter 3

Unlocking the Secrets of Body Language

I touched on body language very briefly in the last chapter, but we are going to address the subject in more detail here. In doing so, you are about to learn a few interesting secrets as well. Before we get going, check out these facts on body language.

- Research shows that whatever we're feeling first shows up in our body and only (nanoseconds) later enters our conscious minds (Lenhardt, 2016).
- A woman has a wider-ranging peripheral vision, which allows her to check out a man's body from head to toe without getting caught. A male's

peripheral vision is poorer, which is why a man will move his gaze up and down a woman's body in a very obvious way. Men do not "ogle" more than women—their tunnel vision means they just get caught more easily (Lenhart, 2016).

- When two people talk to each other, they normally speak toe to toe. If one person turns his feet slightly away or repeatedly moves one foot in an outward direction, this is a strong sign of disagreement, and they want to leave. In fact, the feet and legs are the body parts most likely to reveal a person's true intentions (Lenhardt, 2016).

Body language is a topic that has been extensively researched and continues to be the subject of many social and scientific studies. These fields of research are called kinesics and seek to reveal as much as possible about non-verbal communication. First, let me define the term, and then we can address body language in detail. As per Merriam-Webster's definition, body language is: "The gestures, movements, and mannerisms by which a person or animal communicates with others" (Merriam-Webster, n.d.).

Notice how animal communication is included. We obviously won't be looking at that part of body language, but it is interesting that, as humans, we share a lot of communication techniques that exclude the verbal element.

Mehrabian's Communication Theory

Albert Mehrabian (Ph.D.), a professor and researcher at the University of California, developed a theory that breaks body language down into three percentage-defined categories (Mehrabian, 1971):

- Seven percent of messages pertaining to feelings and attitudes are in the words that are spoken.
- Thirty-eight percent of messages pertaining to feelings and attitudes are paralinguistic (the way that the words are said).
- Fifty-five percent% of messages pertaining to feelings and attitudes are facial expressions.

Mehrabian's theory is also known as the "7–38–55%" rule, and by looking at the percentage breakdowns, it is easy to understand why we argue with people based on the way they say things and their demeanor. The same goes for any type of interaction; not only an argument but serious, light-hearted, frivolous, or instructional conversations too. Considering that our bodies play such a huge role in communication, we need to know how to read body language. By understanding the way that you use your hands when you talk, or the way you sit, or the way you make eye contact, you can make changes to your body language in an effort to become better at overall communication.

How to Read Body Language

First, we need to separate the types of body language, so we can isolate the parts that, when used together, form the entire non-verbal communication set. Gestures come in three main types:

1. Adaptors
2. These are touching and movement behaviors that indicate internal feelings. Shrugging one's shoulders would

indicate not knowing the answer to a question, for instance.

3. Emblems
4. A thumbs up would usually be an emblem of agreement.
5. A middle finger is also an emblem. It conveys anger towards someone.
6. Illustrators
7. Hand gestures to explain something that does not have a universally agreed upon meaning. For example, using your hands to mimic a movement or illustrate a shape, distance, or direction.

We can then separate hand movements and posture, such as a wave to a friend or sitting arms folded to convey seriousness or stoicism. Eye contact is the obvious one, and from observing eye contact, we can detect interest or lack thereof but also use it as a signal to talk, or stop talking, or look a certain way. Then comes our facial expressions—a picture speaks a thousand words—and the pictures that we display on our faces show happiness, sadness, frustration, disgust, anger, fear, and all the rest.

Kinesics studies the above four parts of body language separately, i.e., gestures, hand movements and posture, eye contact, and facial expressions, separately, but we must remember that they work in conjunction with each other.

Clusters of Three

Try to observe three signs in someone's body language before coming to a conclusion. For instance, a surprised facial expression, eye contact, and a shrug of the shoulders could indicate a lack of understanding or surprise at why someone did something or why an incident took place in the way that it did. A shrug on its own may have been interpreted as disinterest, but combined with the surprised expression and eye contact, the sum total becomes an indication of surprise.

Context

Misunderstandings frequently occur due to one party having taken part in a conversation out of context. It may be the verbal or non-verbal part of the conversation, but on the latter, a sarcastic quip could be accompanied by a silly expression and an eye-roll for effect to convey that what has been said is not serious. If you were to say something that was meant to be funny but stared straight into the other person's eyes with a heavy frown and spoke in a monotone voice, you are creating a very different context than in the sarcasm instance.

Congruence

Congruence describes what you hear as matching what you see. If someone tells you that they are really angry but they have a big smile on their face, the link between the two is incongruent. However, this may again be sarcasm creeping in, so it is possible to make an error of judgment. Generally, a facial expression should match what is being said.

Cultural Differences

I told you that you would learn some interesting things about body language, and you are about to do so. In Bulgaria, shaking one's head does not mean no —that could be a confusion-causing gesture. The Chinese look into each other's eyes when they are angry, and in several African cultures, averting one's eyes is a sign of respect. If you are planning to travel to a country different from yours, do some research on body language-related differences.

Positive Versus Negative Body Language

It isn't terribly difficult to spot the difference, but you do get certain people that tend to match negative body language with positive verbal language and vice versa. Let's have a look at some characteristics of good body language first.

1. Sufficient eye contact. You don't have to stare directly into the other person's eyes so vigilantly that you hardly ever break the gaze. A few seconds at a time, followed by a momentary glance away or down, will definitely convey interest in what the person is saying.

2. Good posture. Aside from the fact that good posture is important to maintain to look after our bodies when we age, a person sitting or standing up straight and tall gives off a positive image.

3. Firm handshakes. A decent grip and a firm squeeze are indicators of poise and confidence. In fact, strengthening your handshake, if need be, is a positive step toward being more confident. When you

appear confident, it becomes easier to build on that perceived confidence to spill over into other areas of communication.

4. Genuine smiles. When someone's laughter lines are visible, and they smile with their eyes, then you know it is genuine. Smiling attracts the attention of others, often subconsciously.

5. Standing at close quarters. Standing or sitting close to someone is a sign that you are comfortable around them... not too close though, unless it is a romantic situation. Otherwise, comfortable becomes uncomfortable.

You could say that negative body language is the complete opposite. It is to a degree, but a bit more detail is required. Here we have some characteristics of bad body language.

1. Too much or too little eye contact. The latter is considered rude (not in all cultures). It can convey a lack of interest but can also be the result of social anxiety, meaning that although it may

come across as negative, it isn't intended that way. Too much eye contact can make the other person uncomfortable and can also be used as a tactic to attempt to mask lies. Minimal eye contact is associated with being untruthful, and when lying, we tend to exaggerate eye contact to make us appear to be telling the truth.

2. Crossed arms or legs. These actions put across a message of lack of interest or disdain. This could be observed when someone does not want to participate in a conversation. Some may argue that it is a case of indirect directness. However, for the most part, crossed arms or legs are negative displays.

3. Exaggerated or excessive nodding. Sometimes, it feels like a person is droning on and that you have taken their point. On occasions like this, nodding frequently and quickly could be a sign that they must get on with it. The other interpretation is that the "nodder" is nervous and lacks confidence. Again, this is probably not coming from a bad

place but it is still something to be
aware of.

4. Frowning is an obvious sign of confusion,
   and may also point towards uneasiness,
   or judgmental thoughts. This is a tough
   one to swallow.

5. Fidgeting. This would include looking
   around too. We do this when we are
   nervous or disinterested. Some people
   fidget as a general habit, but in times of
   nervousness or disinterest, the fidgeting
   can become frequent and more
   pronounced.

Other parts of communication are mixed. A raised voice conveys anger, but it is not so much the words that are spoken but the way in which they are spoken. The same could be said for breathing. Deep breaths and speech through clenched teeth could be due to frustration, while calm, relaxed breathing is probably due to a feeling of comfort in the company of others or another.

Open Versus Closed Body Language

Open is generally positive while closed hints towards the negative. Think about it, when you are relaxing at home on the couch, your body language is open and... well, relaxed. Further examples of open body language are:

- Arms open and hands moving with open palms is non-threatening.
- A tilted head is considered an open gesture that expresses interest or curiosity.
- Raised eyebrows and opening one's mouth are signs of genuine appreciation for what is being said.
- Smiling shows warmth and openness.

Closed body language would include the following:

- Crossed arms and legs of disinterest.
- Tapping your finger on the table or tapping your foot on the floor are indicators of impatience or frustration.

- Frowning is most often associated with closed body language but is not always a negative communication trait. It can be a sign of interest in a serious or controversial conversation, although it may also mean anger or being upset.
- Arms down but across the chest and/or torso could be shyness or nervousness as a collateral of social anxiety.

Facial Expressions

Now that we know the differences between positive and negative, as well as open or closed body language, we can get more specific about the areas of our face that contribute to non-verbal communication.

The Eyes

Blinking rapidly can show attraction to another person, but it also highlights the mental processing of something we have just heard. The pupils arguably reveal the most, but sometimes we don't even notice the change from dilated to constricted or vice-versa. Pupils dilate (become bigger) when we see something or someone that we like, and they constrict when we see something or someone that we do not like or have animosity towards.

Eye movements can be broken down quite specifically as follows:

- looking left
- left and down = trying to recall facts
- left and straight = self-conversation before re-engaging
- looking right
- right and down = self-doubt
- right and up = lying
- right and straight = activates the imagination
- glancing
- basically, a sideways look when something catches your peripheral attention
- widened eyes
- shock, surprise, or disbelief
- winking
- accentuation of a joke or a cheeky comment

Covering one's eyes is usually to do with having made a mistake or feeling shocked or disgusted by something rude or disrespectful that has been said. The eyebrow lift is a long-distance "hello" and can be accompanied by a nod of the head. In closer contact, raising one's brow is often a subconscious sign to look at one's face for clearer signals.

The Mouth

Smiling is probably the first thing that most people think of in a mouth-related body language context. The muscle associated with smile activation is called the zygomaticus major and correlates with how much happiness we experience, while watching television or films (Knapp and Hall, 2014). But this can be faked, and one can be caught out because a fake smile does not activate orbicularis oculi movement, more commonly known as eyelid closure. The term "fake" when it comes to smiling is subjective because flashing a smile for a photograph does not always mean that you are faking happiness. It could be that you are having a perfectly good time but are in a serious conversation at a party before you are interrupted for a pic.

A half smile is a sign that someone has gotten away with a lie or has successfully tricked someone. You could also term it a smug type of smile. A slight smile while maintaining eye contact is seductive in nature, while a closed-mouth smile is submissive. A smile accompanied by a wink could be flirtatious or cheeky, and an obviously forced smile sometimes shows disdain.

Now that you know the various types of smiles, you can see what they look like by observing others. For good measure, here are a few interesting facts about smiles:

- Subordinates smile more when their superiors or other people of high status are around.
- Women are 26% more likely to return a smile from a man (Pease, 2017).
- The thought of others, say, family or friends, when you are by yourself is likely to make you smile.
- In social encounters, women smile 87% of the time, and men smile 67% of the time (Pease, 2017).
- Athletes have been observed to display smiles in sizes proportionate to finishing first, second, third, or further back.

The mouth is not only about smiles, lip gestures have a lot to reveal as well. Here are ten common ones to look out for and what they mean:

1. Pursed lips/sucking your lips is a show of stress, or holding back a facial expression, such as trying not to laugh when it would be inappropriate. Sometimes when smiling at a work colleague in a passage, we purse our lips.

2. The mouth shrug, which looks like an upside-down smile when done in conjunction with a shoulder shrug, is a sign of not caring or a lack of interest in a subject. If a frown is added, the unspoken words could be interpreted as "it has nothing to do with me," or "I don't want to hear about that."

3. A down mouth expression, which is a much less exaggerated version of the mouth shrug; conveys dejection or disappointment. Becoming tense and irritated are also characterized by this time of expression.

4. Lower lip biting is pretty much instinctual, and we will not notice ourselves doing it unless we are specifically looking out for it. A gentle lip bite is associated with sexual attraction and seduction. The biological reason is

that the act draws more blood flow to our lips, making them redder. A more continuous biting motion may reveal that you are trying to stop yourself from saying something that could be construed as rude or of an inciting nature.

5. Upper lip biting is less common, so upon careful observation of conjunctive indicators such as raised eyebrows or constricted pupils, a conclusion of nerves or anxiety is a likely one.

6. The good old pucker-up that your grandma gives you on your birthday means something different on non-grandma-and-birthday-related occasions. Women use the pucker-up or pout gesture as a manipulative move that can come out when they don't get their way. Men also use the pucker-up/pout, but research has revealed that women employ it way more often than men do (Navarro and Karlins, 2015).

7. Bulging lips occur when we push air out through our lips while they are tightly closed. This is an aggressive gesture and

can be traced back in an evolutionary sense to primates who make the bulging lip motion before attacking (Navarro and Karlins, 2015).

8. Lip quivering is an indicator of fear and can be joined by tears in the face of something frightening.

9. If you suck in your lips, there is a large possibility that you are experiencing large amounts of anxiety. Studies have linked sucking in the lips to individuals who are grieving (Pease, 2017).

10. Parting lips can be instinctual and has been interpreted as either flirtatious or an indicator that you wish to begin speaking.

Now that we have looked at smile and lip gestures, let's jump inside the mouth and examine what motions and movements our tongues make and what they mean in non-verbal communication.

- Licking the lips is a sign of attraction— the "licking your lips due to hunger" expression is more of an expression than an involuntary sign. We do also lick our lips in times of stress, so it is a confusing bit of body language to discern.

- Rubbing the upper lip with the tongue is associated with positive emotions and happens when we receive good news.
- Sticking your tongue out is generally a playful act or when we realize we have done something silly.
- Concentration on difficult tasks often brings with it a tongue that is slightly stuck out to the side of the mouth.
- Teeth licking is a sign of aggression and stems from our teeth being a primitive weapon (Navarro and Karlins, 2015).

Our mouths, and especially our breathing, can combine with air gestures that can reveal fear, relief, or accomplishment, to list a few. A small gasp happens when we are upset or feeling deflated, while a large gasp is suited to a moment of shock or amazement. A loud air sigh could mean relief when something is over, and an exhale with puffed-up cheeks tells people that a stressful moment has passed or something potentially disastrous has been avoided. To state the obvious, whistling indicates joy, happiness, and excitement, or is used to get attention, often the attention of your dog. Here is a quick look at some of the other mouth gestures:

- mouth stretching = fear
- mouth open = pain (in addition to what was discussed above)
- yawning = boredom, tiredness, and even a nervous reaction on occasion
- one-sided mouth raise = contempt

As you can imagine, there are several combinations of facial expressions and gestures which go along with words and other body movements. I hope you noticed that a fair amount of body language is subconscious, as is the ability to identify the different types of body language.

Microexpressions

These types of facial expressions last less than four seconds and cannot be faked. Microexpressions are completely natural reactions to a trigger or even that we cannot help.

- A surprised expression involves raised, curved eyebrows that stretch the skin below. Horizontal wrinkles develop across the forehead, and eyelids are opened to reveal the white of the eye. The jaw drops, and it looks as if one's mouth would have fallen to the floor if it was not attached. If you hear something that seems almost unbelievable or you find out some amazing news that was unforeseen, you will be microexpressing surprise in no time.

- Fear induces raised and drawn-together eyebrows, most often in a straight line. Unlike surprise, fear limits wrinkles to the middle of the forehead. The top eyelids are raised, and the lower lid/s are tensed up, revealing the upper white and hiding the lower white. The lips are tense like the lower eyelids and the mouth will probably be slightly open. Being accosted by a mugger would immediately send our face into fear of microexpression.

- Disgust sees the narrowing of the eyes and a raised lip that exposes the top row of teeth. The nose becomes wrinkled, and the cheeks are raised. This could happen if we are squeamish and witness something "blood and gutsy" or if someone tells us an offensive joke.

- Lowered, drawn-together eyebrows, accompanied by vertical lines between the eyes, along with a tensed lip and an intense stare, are visible when anger is triggered. It is also common to notice flaring nostrils and an extension of the jaw when we find ourselves angry over an insult or an immediately regrettable act.

- Happiness in its pure instantaneous form cannot be faked. A happy microexpression includes the big smile, raised cheeks, outer nose to outer lip wrinkle, and crow's feet outside the eyes —okay, let's call them laughter lines.

- Sadness causes a lower lip pout, a raised jaw, and drawn-in corners of the inner eyebrow. Bad news, a melancholy scene in a movie, or a particular song are some of the causes of the sad microexpression.

- Contrary to popular belief, the hate/contempt/detest microexpression is pretty asymmetrical, with only a slightly raised corner of the lip. This would happen if you came across an enemy or heard a narrow-minded and stupid opinion.

The Gesture/Posture Crossover

The glaringly obvious example of a gesture is pointing. If there is loud music on and you want to draw someone's attention to something, you would tap them on the shoulder and point—simple. It gets a tiny bit more complicated, and there is a fair few more gestures than the point. Also, they can work in conjunction with posture, and changes in posture. Technically, *posture* falls under *gestures*, but I like to separate them so we can see how they interact with each other.

- Finger steepling
- You know what I mean. Fingers and thumbs touch but spaced wide apart so the palms face each other.
- This "gest-post" sends a message of control and order and is often observed in people with positions of power (boss, politician, speaker, etc.)

- Pulling your ear
- This is also heavily subconscious. Not all of us do it, but when we are thinking about something, like an answer to a difficult question, we pull our ears while trying to come up with the answer. The same applied to touching your cheek.
- Hair twisting/twirling
- Most of us know the connotations of attraction associated with hair twisting or twirling, but in a formal setting such as a job interview, it aligns more with nervousness.
- Rubbing your eyes
- "I can't believe my eyes," is the linked phrase. The symbolism reflects the reality of hearing something that is very difficult to believe or take in.
- Rubbing your nose
- This is also an indicator of untruths.
- An interesting fact about this is that very often, after a handshake, we will instinctively touch our noses (Semin, 2015).
- Pinching the bridge of your nose.

- Combined with a head tip, you are silently saying that you are making negative assumptions about what is being said.
- Hands clenched together.
- It can be a sign of relaxation but is often mixed up with an attempt to hold yourself back based on frustration.

Walking briskly shows confidence, while shuffling or walking slowly with poor posture are signs of dejection and lack of self-confidence. Displaying thumbs shows dominance and aggression while clasping hands behind the back can precede an angry outburst.

These are not all hard and fast rules, but now that you have some deeper knowledge of gestures and posture, you can start looking out for them in yourself and others.

Pacifying

Studies have shown that in an attempt to restore itself to "normal conditions," the brain will enlist the body to provide comforting behaviors. In other words, the brain requires the body to do something that will stimulate nerve endings to release calming endorphins in the brain so the brain can be soothed (Starla, 2023).

Pacifying behaviors are quite a personal thing, and you may see people rubbing their shoulders gently, scratching their necks, jiggling their feet (if sitting down), or rubbing the tops of their thighs. The more you get to know someone, the easier it is to identify their pacifying behavior traits.

Haptics

Haptic communication is through touch and can be as innocuous as a tap on the shoulder to get someone's attention to a punch in the face out of anger. Sometimes, touch is forced or unavoidable, and sometimes it is unwelcome. Here are some examples:

- Professional
- Dentistry or physiotherapy requires touch.
- Greeting
- Handshake, hug, kiss, high five, or other.
- Guiding
- Holding someone's arm as they walk down a flight of stairs.

- Punishment
- A smack or a punch.
- Sympathy
- An arm around the shoulder or a hug.
- Gaining attention
- This would include the innocuous tap on the shoulder.

Blocking

If you are in a situation that makes you uncomfortable, you are likely to adjust your positioning to something closed off as a means of blocking. Essentially, the act of blocking is putting up a silent barrier by crossing our arms or legs. Raised eyebrows and a head tilt are more passive types of blocking, as well as an open-handed shoulder shrug. The complete "shut the door immediately" block is turning your back and walking away.

Paralanguage

Changes in pitch, tempo, or fluency of one's voice are what qualify as paralanguage. Basically, the parts of spoken language that do not involve words. Yes, words are being spoken, but it is the way in which they are being spoken that makes up the paralanguage. Raising the volume of your voice could indicate urgency, while lowering it to a whisper could indicate a threat. Sarcasm employs paralanguage in that emphasis on a word in a sentence will identify that a statement is sarcastic and not serious. Hesitations, pauses, long "um's," and stumbling over words are also paralanguage that can be interpreted in a plethora of ways depending on the circumstance. In music, they say that the pauses between the notes are as important as the notes themselves—the same is the case with language and (parts of) paralanguage.

Emblem Gestures

Many of these are the same worldwide, like the thumbs up, or a wave. The thumb and forefinger touch, with the other three fingers up means "all good," or "okay," and the fist bump is a sign of congratulations. There are some variances, and this category is very wide. Have a game of charades and note how many emblem gestures are on display.

Mirroring

There are many definitions of mirroring, also called "limbic synchrony," and to a degree, it is obvious, but this definition is one that I like for its simplicity (Van Edwards, n.d.):

Mirroring, also known as mimicking or Gauchais Reaction, is a nonverbal technique where a person copies the body language, vocal qualities, or attitude of another person. It is usually done subconsciously and can indicate interest or even attraction. Mirroring can occur many times throughout a social interaction and often goes unnoticed.

The definition tells us that mirroring is usually subconscious, but think back to the previous chapter when I dealt with purposeful mimicking to show attraction. My point is that the lessons we take from subconscious mirroring, can be applied in a conscious manner for our own benefit. Let's have a look at the subconscious first, and then I will explain how conscious mirroring can be seen as passive manipulation.

- Fronting
- Standing directly in front of the other person, a comfortable distance apart, and

maintaining eye contact for a few seconds, letting the eyes wander, then back to direct eye contact. Both people in this scenario will feel that they are important to each other for the duration of the interaction.

- The triple nod
- This does two important things. First, research shows that when you do the triple nod, the other person will speak three to four times longer, making them feel listened to and important. Second, when you nod, you are basically agreeing with what the other person is saying, and this builds what scientists call a "yes set" (Pease, 2017).
- Pace and volume
- During a conversation, you can establish comfort, and very often, warmth, by speaking at the same pace and volume as your counterpart.
- Obviously, screaming matches or arguments don't fall on the "establishing comfort" side of the fence but also qualify as mirroring.

The same applies to using the same words for expression, as well as mirroring hand gestures and facial expressions, which takes us more toward mimicry. If you go into a business meeting with stark awareness of body language and intend to use it to close a deal, then there is a bit of manipulation going on. I referred to it as passive because you don't want the other person or people in the meeting to realize. It could be disingenuous. I don't know. I'll let you make your mind up.

For a bit of fun, here is what I believe to be an untested theory that you might like to try. I would advise only single people to try this out. Sit in a coffee shop, look around, and find someone that you would want to ask out on a date. Don't stare at them but take note of what they do, and mimic that movement a few seconds after they do it. If that person changes seating position, do the same. If they run a hand through their hair, then copy that. When they have a sip of their drink, have a quick pause and take a sip of your drink. After repeating this for ten minutes or so, then go up to that person and ask if they would like company or if they would like to join you... positive results should be expected. As I said, not actually tested, but some food for thought and maybe a chance to fall in love. Good luck!

Mistakes, Tips, and Tricks

When I say tricks, I don't mean in a nefarious way, but to conclude the section on body language, here are some quickfire points to keep in mind:

- firm (not too firm) handshakes
- don't nod excessively
- remember someone's name
- don't stand too close
- avoid overly exaggerated gestures
- don't look at your watch or phone
- remember that body language etiquette may differ depending on where you are
- stand up straight
- maintain interest
- don't interrupt

The last tip deserves a bullet point of its own:

- SMILE

It is hard to receive a smile and not automatically return it... and on we march towards how to become a small talker of acclaim.

Chapter 4

Be Great at Small Talk

Small talk is a strange phenomenon. In one sense, it is fodder to fill a gap when interacting with someone that you feel awkward around. The level of awkwardness depends on your level of social anxiety. The exchange of "Hello, how are you?" and "I'm fine thanks, and you?" are completely different when said to a shop attendant or cashier, as opposed to a close friend or family member. It sounds terrible, and the truth can be harsh, but if you check into a hotel for one night as a break from a long drive, you don't genuinely care about how the check-in clerk is doing and whether they have had a good day or not. However, the polite thing to do is ask, then answer, get the check-in done, and wish them a good day.

I do have to include a disclaimer and say that many people, usually extroverts and those with natural charisma, really do care. There is nothing unusual about getting past the pleasantries and then asking questions of the check-in clerk about their hobbies or family and creating a genuine discussion beyond the realm of small talk. It is difficult to say if there are more *small-talk-then-walk*, or *small-talk-to-full-conversation* types out there, but I am almost certain that everyone has experienced being suddenly left with one person at a party and standing in silence while both of you wrack your brains for something to say. I am hoping that we can change that with this crash course chapter on small talk supremacy.

The Science

As we know, scientists study pretty much anything, and the non-scientists around should be happy. Knowledge is power and the more knowledge that science gives us, the better we can become as humans. Small talk is no different, so I'd like to cover a bit of the science and then dive into the practical side of an uncomfortable chat, that you will soon be able to turn into something comfortable and enjoyable.

Interpersonal Synchronization

Also called interpersonal coordination, explains that "it feels like I've known you for longer" feeling. We probably associate this more with romantic relationships, and that would not be incorrect, but it also works with friendship. Like-mindedness comes into play. Imagine you are at a work function, with partners invited, making it a possible minefield of awkwardness. If someone is wearing a football jersey of your favorite club, a conversation may spark immediately, as you realize that your fandom is similar. The discussion slides naturally to music—you are astounded that the other person likes the same artists that you do, and so it carries on.

In a study published in the Social Cognitive and Affective Neuroscience journal in 2020, this phenomenon was explained as follows (Heggli et al., 2020):

The familiarity has its roots in interpersonal synchronization, where speech rhythms, walking patterns, and even breathing match with those of others simply from our shared perceptions that we notice as we acquaint ourselves with each other.

Neural coupling is a term that further explains that our brains sync with each other during storytelling sessions. A Princeton University study established this through MRI monitoring during discussions and talks in storytelling format. The study was called *Brain to Brain Coupling: A Mechanism for Creating and Sharing a Social World*, and was published in 2012 on the National Library of Medicine Biotechnology Website.

To summarize the findings, it became apparent that small talk strategies and techniques could be learned in a way that would manifest as a transition to deeper and more meaningful conversations (Hasson et al., 2012).

Time to stray from the science into the practicality of it all.

Why Is Small Talk Necessary?

Firstly, it can relieve awkwardness, and when learned in the correct or most effective manner, small talk can be very useful in alleviating social anxiety and improving conversations. Anyone would choose interesting and fulfilling interactions over boring and awkward ones. If that is to be achieved, then small talk is absolutely, positively necessary. In addition, skills in this area help to strengthen relationships, build connections socially and professionally, create confidence, and make us feel good about ourselves— and the most introverted of introverts can achieve these milestones.

How to Use Small Talk

A little preparation goes a long way. If you are going to dinner with one person you know and some of their friends who you have never met, you are well placed to make some good small talk for two reasons. First, your friend is mutual, and that can lead to conversations about where you know that friend from. It is easy for a conversation like that to flow. Second, your friend is a resource for information on his or her other friends. If you can find out some of the things that the friends enjoy, like hobbies perhaps, then you are armed with something that you can bring up if the conversation is taking strain.

I tend to stray away from actually practicing what I am going to say word for word, but it is not a bad tactic. However, you do want to avoid coming across as someone who has memorized what to say. There has to be a natural limit to it, but also bear in mind that often, small talk starts out mechanically and transforms into a natural state. The typical route from the start of a conversation through small talk and to a more meaningful discussion is as follows:

1. Greet the other person and exchange pleasantries.
2. Ask an open-ended question: "How long have you known Stan?"
3. Build on the topic.
4. Listen carefully and ask questions at the appropriate time.
5. Express your interest with exclamations like, "oh wow" or "that's awesome.
6. Read body language signals.
7. If the conversation tapers off, then using subject change bridging questions that refer to something that is common knowledge: "Have you seen X, Y, Z movie?"

The rulebook is pliable, so the steps above are not always in that order. For instance, number six can come in right from the first handshake, but sometimes we will forget to observe if we are nervous. As the nerves settle and comfort sets in, body language signs will become more obvious.

What to Say and What Not to Say

As a matter of interest, individuals on the autism spectrum tend to be very literal and struggle to understand what is socially inappropriate. In order to have a successful small-talk session, you need to be appropriate, and to do so, there are some subjects that should be avoided. Let's first take a look at some good topics and then some bad ones.

The absolutely obvious ones are the weather, current events, movies or TV, books, hobbies, food, work, and family. Sports are also an often used small-talk opener, in addition to mutual friends and music, but here is a comprehensive list:

- travel
- schools you attend
- where you grew up
- best advice you were given
- guilty pleasures
- If you could meet anyone, who would it be?

At this stage, you are making some progress with topics that will very possibly lead to "big chat." On we go.

- pets
- What made you choose your career?
- Tell me more about your job.
- embarrassing moments
- best childhood memories
- whether you consider yourself an introvert or extrovert

As the small talk becomes "big talk," you can move on to subjects that become appropriate but that would not have been appropriate earlier on in the conversation. I want to make sure there is no confusion, so I will list the *inappropriate* topics:

- sex
- politics
- religion

Those are the trifecta of bad conversation starters. Let's press on...

- family trauma
- finances (always a big NO)
- hygiene
- bodily fluids
- sensitive social issues

- jokes that could be construed as offensive
- bad-mouthing other people (you should try to avoid this in all cases)

You will gauge the best topics as the conversation flows, and no matter how socially awkward, we all have some sort of natural ability to sense the way a discussion will go.

According to socialself.com, the following are the nine best small-talk questions of all time (Sander, 2020). They are subjective, of course, but well worth a look:

1. How do you know the people here?
2. What do you do for fun?
3. What is your favorite way to start the day?
4. What do you like to do outside of work?
5. What kind of TV shows or movies do you like best?
6. What do you like to do on weekends?
7. Where are you originally from?
8. What type of music do you like?
9. What is your favorite food?

If I am to be ultra-critical of Viktor Sander, questions one, four, and six are kind of the same. We are, however, not here to criticize but to learn, so all in all —good questions.

Context will often lead to the types of questions you are asking and then answering. The people you are talking to may do the same, as well as the venue, the occasion, and even the weather. In light of this, here are some suggestions for topics in different contexts.

- First time meeting someone
- Are you enjoying yourself?
- What is the reason you came to this event?
- Was it difficult to get here?
- Do you know many people here?
- What do you do for work?
- For networking purposes (at a conference, perhaps)
- What made you decide to come to this conference?
- What line of work are you in?
- Did you go to college to study in pursuance of your career?
- What was your first job?
- Do you have any specific work goals?

- Conversations with kids
- What is your favorite subject at school?
- Who is your favorite teacher?
- What do you want to be when you grow up?
- What is your best friend's name?
- Would you like to tell me a bit about him or her?
- First date
- Have you been on any disastrous dates?
- Do you come here often?
- If you could meet any celebrity, who would it be?
- What is your pet peeve?
- How did you meet your best friend?
- At a bar
- What are you drinking?
- Do you come here often? (I hope you have noticed that this one keeps cropping up).
- Who did you come here with?
- I like your shirt, where did you get it from?
- Do you know _____ insert name?
- With friends
- How are things going at work?

- Did you listen to that song I suggested?
- How are your parents?
- Do you want to go to the beach?
- These are the easiest questions because they are for people who you are already comfortable with.
- Funny
- What is your shower song?
- Tell me an embarrassing story.
- What is the worst wardrobe malfunction you have ever had?
- What is the most terrible joke that you have ever heard?
- Have you seen any good stand-up comedy lately?

You should be able to tell that the questions under each section have the ability to kick off good and productive discussions. Your intuition will guide you, but if you land on a subject where there is a common interest, then the conversation will flow naturally, allowing you to relax and enjoy yourself.

Becoming Better at Small Talk

As a possible introvert, improving at small talk can open so many doors. What you are about to read are conventions that will put you outside your comfort zone. But first, a quote from an unexpected source. Roy T. Bennett, who died in 2018, is a former Zimbabwean politician but also a linguist who wrote a book, *The Light in Your Heart: Inspirational Thoughts for Living Your Best Life.*

The comfort zone is a psychological state in which one feels familiar, safe, at ease, and secure. You never change your life until you step out of your comfort zone; change begins at the end of your comfort zone (graciousquotes, 2022).

Be More Social

Think about it this way: When you learn how to play the guitar, you have to concentrate hard and really stare at the strings to make sure your finger lands in the correct place. When you have done that thousands of times, you don't have to look so intently. Thus, you are more relaxed and playing becomes more fun. Sociability isn't much different. You will be uncomfortable and awkward, just like when you hold a guitar for the first time and become used to the feel. The more you socialize, the more instinctual it becomes, meaning that you don't have to put as much thought in, and you can have more fun in social environments.

Be Prepared to Listen

Make a concerted effort to listen intently to what people say. Even if you are part of a conversation involving several people and you don't say anything at all, you will still adapt to comfort in silence. If it is a one-on-one conversation, you can encourage the other person to talk more by saying that you find them interesting or that they mentioned something that you would like them to expand. You should start to feel more comfortable and the other person will appreciate the interest you are taking.

Model Your Conversation Style on Someone Else

Back to the guitar scenario. Often, you will see a musician playing, and it reminds you of another musician, possibly from a previous era. There is a good chance that there has been some influence and style modeling. If you like a person's conversation style and disposition, you want to add elements to your conversation etiquette without being a clone of the other person.

Bad First

The best surfer in the world was bad in the beginning, so was the best golfer, and the best pianist. The best accountant was once bad, and the best bartender was also bad. You have to be bad at something before you become good at it. Remember that if you truly want to become a better conversationalist, pushing yourself into a place that is comfortable will help tremendously.

Some Mistakes to Avoid

If you know what type of mistakes you could make, then you can put measures in place to, well, not make them.

Assuming That Nobody Wants to Talk to You

Every single person is interesting to some other people. Not all people. Just take popular culture. You find some comedians funny and others not. You have your favorite songs and songs that annoy you. A TV show that you find boring is of great interest to the next person, and the fact that you don't like the beach is absolutely fine. Don't fear that you won't be funny, interesting, or entertaining. You may not be those things to a person that you end up talking to, and the feeling is probably mutual, but don't let that fear prohibit you from starting or participating in discussions.

Interrupting or Intruding

If you are socially awkward, you may be too enthusiastic to say something and just blurt it out as an interruption. If it happens, you have time to apologize but try to prevent it. Although it is a mistake to avoid, they do happen. Also, you don't want to be jumping into a conversation that you aren't really part of. So, get your timing right!

Start Talking Without Having Anything to Say

If you walk up to someone with the intention of starting a conversation, then you should have something to say. Remember, that if you initiate a chat, it should be your goal to make the other person feel comfortable. Introducing yourself and then falling silent can be a bit embarrassing, but this should not happen to you, considering that you have access to all the opening small talk questions and comments.

Being Controversial

There is a large potential for awkwardness if you throw out an opinion on a controversial topic and the other participants have opposing views. I'm not saying that a healthy discussion about points of disagreement is not possible, but raising something controversial is not wise to do just after you have exchanged names.

Being Hard to Follow

If you are talking to older people, you should probably speak slowly and avoid conversation pieces about things that they are unaware of. I am going to use an obvious example here, but a full-on conversation about cryptocurrency or AI is bound to make things awkward and uncomfortable.

Talking Too Much About Yourself

Under this category, we can add "talking too much to the other person" because if you are asking questions to the point that you can see the other person getting uncomfortable, you should shift the focus to a story or an anecdote. Talking about yourself in a way that you are dominating the conversation will give off a self-absorbed vibe and is not a great tactic. You are looking for a conversation where the other party has a chance to equally participate.

Wasting Someone's Time

Initiating a conversation and then looking at your phone or your watch or looking down would be disrespectful to the other participant. Their inner feelings would probably be that they don't understand why you would start a conversation and immediately lose interest. It is a different ball game if you are mutually unable to avoid a conversation, but even though there is no distinct initiator, both parties should aim to be present.

Deeper Conversations

I guess we could call this the goal or the finish line, but we can't forget that we have to take some steps to get there. Not every small-talk situation will travel the path to deep conversation, and oftentimes, there is just no possibility that it will happen. That is perfectly okay, but if you are at the point where you would like to guide the discussion into deeper waters, then there are some tactics you can apply. Your pre-small talk goal could have been to take the conversation deep, even though it hadn't started. Either way, the following should help the process along, whether from the beginning or further down the line.

- Introductions
- Keep them short and vary them according to the context.

- Don't be too generic.
- Skip the questions that you know the other person has heard many times. The variety tends to create comfort early - not always, but often the case.
- Ask questions that make the other party interested and excited.
- I mentioned doing research. This is a scenario where some research would help. When you ask someone questions about their favorite hobby, you can establish comfort sooner.
- Have three good stories.
- If you are struggling with continuity, you can tell a story. Having three to choose from expounds on the benefits of variety.
- Simple riddles can be particularly enjoyable and can also promote laughter and relaxation.
- Take note of things you have in common or experiences that you both have been through.
- Colloquially, it is referred to as the "same here" moment. We all know the one.

In a general sense, you want to distance yourself

from the norm. Small talk will be more memorable if you have some quirks or idiosyncrasies that shine through naturally. It really does boil down to circumstance—some small-talk experiences are not destined for further development, but many are destined for deeper, more meaningful conversation, and hence, connections.

Don't be scared to ask questions, but put in some work at the art of asking. Stay tuned.

Chapter 5

The Art of the Ask

The cliches are, "if you don't ask, you don't get," and "ask and you will receive," among others. Naquib Mahfouz added some meat to the bones when he wrote: "You can tell whether a man is clever by his answers. You can tell whether a man is wise by his questions" (Johnson-Davies, 2006).

In an eloquent way, he is saying that we must ask the right questions to provoke thoughtful and meaningful conversation. But why do we want to have these deeper conversations? For growth would be the answer. Also, for fulfillment, and the strengthening of human connection and relationships. It is more than just having something to talk about, and if we again turn to science and a specific 2017 study, the above points are reinforced.

The study I am referring to revealed that when we feel completely safe with someone, our nervous system relaxes in a way that invites healing and growth (Mercado and Hibel, 2017). I would argue that healing and growth are valuable as human beings, but how and why do we get there? Let's start with the "why" first.

- Asking questions makes you more likable.
- It conveys interest, as we know, and the other party will feel some sense of flattery that you genuinely want to know about them and their lives.
- Don't jump right in and start asking about someone's life hardships near the start of the chat.
- Think about the way in which someone confessing their hardships makes you feel. That's it.
- Learning
- Asking questions allows you to learn about another person, and again, it doesn't have to get deep immediately.

- Logically, one of the first questions would be, "what is your name?" That is not a deep question but a necessary one to get the discussion going.
- It is scientific... kind of.
- I don't mean scientific as in research-based, but rather the approach.
- Science tends to collect data, analyze it, and conclude. A good set of questions facilitates this process.
- Critical thinking
- As a chat gets deeper, opinions may be fingered and thoughts provoked.
- Your views might be challenged as you start thinking about topics that require deeper thought.
- There is a belief that we should not just accept everything but rather give it some critical thought and ask questions.

Questions can also lead to positive change and can result in innovation. Questions spark ideas and have the ability to broaden the mind. I will say it again—knowledge is power, and you gain knowledge by listening. However, you need to ask the question before you listen to the answer.

Traits of a Good Question

If you are a journalist conducting an interview, you want to extract every single detail. The collateral is that you may ask questions that sound stupid or that give the other person the impression that you are stupid or don't have the ability to follow the conversation. Another example would be a lawyer. He or she needs to completely and fully know every single fact, so seemingly stupid questions will crop up. These instances do not point to deep conversation, meaning that there is a wider net into which questions can fall. Whatever the context of questions being asked and answered, clarity, conciseness, and openness must be the aim.

How to Ask a Good Question

In a grocery store, you may ask an employee a question like, "Where would I find the Black Cat peanut butter?" The question is clear and concise, leaving no confusion. You are looking for peanut butter manufactured by Black Cat: interpretation is not required. But not all questions can be that simple. You get some more complex questions, of which there are three broad types.

Open-Ended Questions

Pretty simple, any question that does not have a "yes" or "no" answer. Room for discussion is created by questions such as, "what was it like at boarding school?" or "what did you do on your vacation." The same questions could have been asked in a closed-off way, i.e., "did you enjoy boarding school," or "did you enjoy your vacation." The latter way of asking can still lead to further conversation on the boarding school or vacation experience, but it encourages a one-word answer.

Follow-up Questions

Using the vacation question; the person would tell you a bit about what they did, and you could then pick out a particular part and ask another question. For instance, "oh wow, you went skydiving, what was the plane ride like?" This leads the conversation to flow like water down a mountain stream.

Leading Questions

These types of questions prompt specific responses. They can be closed off but not in a definitive yes/no way. Something like, "didn't you find it really scary just before you jumped out of the plane." For most people, the answer would be yes, and you would then follow up by asking the person to tell you more.

Questioning is certainly not always in the above order, and the different types of questions vary depending on context.

Traits of a Good Question Asker

If you were to ask questions in a monotone voice and give the impression that you don't care about the answers and are doing the other person a favor by asking them, you are not going down the path of good question-asking. The questions may be decent questions, but they become almost redundant if you ask them in unproductive ways.

A generic question like, "how was your day," can be turned into a more curious question, such as, "what was the most fun part of your day." The second question takes a deeper plunge without being intrusive. The frivolous becomes more substantial.

Avoid asking just for the sake of it. Put some thought into your questions, and do not be afraid to ask clarifying questions. For an introvert and/or a socially anxious individual, judgment is a big fear, which can lead to the absence of clarifying questions. A question that you perceive to be dumb probably isn't nearly as bad as you think it may be. Something to consider is the need to be respectful. If you think a question may come across in a disrespectful manner, rather keep it aside for future use.

How to Become a Better Question Asker

Some of these have been covered, and others not. The former I will keep short, and the latter I will provide sufficient detail.

- Be a good listener
- We know this one: You need to listen to what the other person is saying so you have the data to ask return questions.
- Don't be scared
- Again, stupid questions don't exist (kind of).
- The thing to remember is that if you don't ask questions for fear of looking stupid, you will wind up confused and will appear more stupid.
- Research
- If you play an instrument, you probably know a fair amount about the instrument

and can talk at length about it. Try and make this the case across several unrelated topics.

- Follow the flow
- You don't need to have a steadfast plan and an order in which you intend to ask questions.
- Just let the conversation take its natural course.
- Accentuate pauses
- We all need time to think, so afford yourself that luxury by extending your pauses. Also, if you ask a question the instant the other party stops talking, it could appear rushed and mechanical— the flow is good.
- Ask questions that promote further discussion
- I'm talking about your open-ended and follow-up questions.
- Keep your questions short
- Avoid something like, "what is your opinion on space travel? If you think it is a good thing then why do you think that? If your opinion is that space travel is bad, please could you explain a bit more?"

- It is too long and convoluted... step by step.
- Get your sequence right
- As I said, the order of questions is not a hard and fast rule, but be sure to get the order right as dictated by the context.
- Appropriate tone
- In a casual sense, a casual tone is fine, but in a job interview, which could be more formal, you need to adjust your tone accordingly.

Types of Questioning

Questions, whether open or close-ended, leading, or follow-up, can be broken down into different question types. Let's have a look at those:

- Superlative questions
- These use words like least favorite, best, worst, scariest, funniest, etc.
- For example, "what was the funniest moment from the dinner you went to last night?" or "what was the worst part of the interstate drive?"
- Challenge questions

- What was the most challenging course that you took in college?
- How did you approach the challenges of training for a marathon?
- What would you say is the biggest challenge for teenagers in present times?
- You can see that the third example is more opinion based than the first two, in that it requires an opinion on something that the person is not involved in or hasn't done personally.
- Situational or sense questions
- Situational would refer to situations that guide your questions (obviously).
- For example, "This is a cool party, how do you know the host?"
- Sense would quite literally mean your senses.
- For example, "Can you smell the coffee? What type of hot drink is your favorite?"
- Past, present, and future questions
- Pretty self-explanatory
- Past, "What did you do last weekend?"
- Present, "What is your function at today's conference?"

- Future, "What are your plans for your vacation?"
- Needs-oriented questions
- These would fit into the customer-service world
- "How can I help you?"
- "Would you like me to get you a drink?"
- These types of questions can become broader, but basically, any question that looks after the needs of another person.

There is also a questioning technique called funneling where you start with a broad question and funnel the conversation with more specific follow-up questions. This is a bit like a lawyer questioning an expert witness, starting with qualifications and funneling down to the crux of the matter.

Some Tips to Get Deeper

As a newly versed good-question answerer, you may be wondering how to get to the phase where you start to connect on a deeper and emotional level with the other person. The transition from acquaintances to friends, or new friends to lovers sums this one up nicely. Some of what follows, leads to the deepest part of the proverbial conversation swimming pool, and some of what follows is transitional between shallow and deep.

- Don't be self-conscious.
- It is going to be a challenge to reach a level of conversation that augurs well for a deeper discussion if you are self-conscious or nervous.
- You need to be brave to approach the deep end.
- Be confident about what you would like to know about the other person.
- Don't forget that these scenarios are most probably not first-meeting ones.
- I'm not saying that they cannot be, but the deepness resulting from the first discussion is less common than in future discussions.
- Confidence does not mean being pushy. If you can sense trepidation or a reluctance to chat about what you are asking, then back off.
- Get your timing right.

- Be mindful of the other person's boundaries. You should be able to get an intuitive sense of what you can and can't ask.
- Say the other person has endured childhood trauma and you reach a point where they have opened up to you about most of what happened, but it starts to seem like they don't want to go further, you should direct the conversation in a different way.
- Thinking about you can reach a level of depth and then retreat with the intention of re-addressing the topic in a future conversation, or later on in the current conversation.
- Have some idea of the answer.
- If you have researched a topic that your new or soon-to-become-friend enjoys talking about, you can ask questions to which you vaguely know the answer. The effort on your part, no matter the contents of the discussion, is a move in the right direction.
- State what you know.

- Perhaps, the other person is a scientist and you have a rough knowledge of their field of research. You can state the things you know and ask for clarity. This category, and the previous one, have a slight overlap, so the same principle applies.
- Open yourself up to weaknesses.
- Science is a "prove me wrong/prove myself wrong" endeavor. You come up with a theory and examine what could be wrong with it. That is why we progress.
- Using this thinking, you can put forward an idea and ask for an opinion, knowing that you may be wrong or that there are sections of your opinion that could be weak. If pointed out to you after you have given the other person room to do so, then you can change your opinion on account of having a better understanding of the topic on the whole.
- If you have a deep conversation about social issues and you have a steadfast stance that you are not prepared to

change, then there is not much point to the conversation.

- Try not to be too vague
- Avoid vague questions to achieve meaningful conversation status. It is okay to start broadly, such as asking someone to tell you about themselves, then narrowing it down using follow up questions triggered by what they say.
- One question at a time
- Self-explanatory: basically, don't ask someone three questions at once. Ask one question and after you get the answer, lead with the next question.
- Listen carefully
- "Sorry, I didn't get that" is not going to suffice.
- If you want to get deep you have to pay deep attention.
- Don't worry about silence
- In a deep conversation about something personal or emotional there may be a need for silence to gain composure.
- In a deep conversation about something controversial, either party may need silence to formulate their thoughts.

- When the silence is not uncomfortable, you have waded into the deep part of the deep end.
- Ask questions in a non-confrontational way
- If you watch two people with opposing views in a formally organized debate, it *should* be polite and respectful.
- You need to apply the same modus to a formal conversation in an informal setting. Being rude and getting personal is going to throw you way back into the shallow end and possibly out of the pool altogether.
- Use conversation-appropriate language
- You may have a large vocabulary. However, big words don't necessarily impress people, and if you confuse your chatting partners. The discussion won't be productive enough to reach a meaningful point.

Good Follow-up Questions

If showing curiosity equals proximity to open up more, which is the case, we can build curiosity in ourselves and the other person by sharpening our follow-up questions. Not asking follow-up questions is like putting on a song and turning it off after the introduction. If you do this and you never get to the verses and chorus, the result will be that you don't really know what the song is about, considering that you have only scratched the surface—you have to ask the questions to assist the conversation in its progression.

Repeating the "why" questions, but not excessively, is a good way to elicit information and gives the advantage of knowing when to stop probing. Getting the answer, "just because," will indicate that the other person is not comfortable sharing more information. On the other hand, asking someone why something happened, and then going further with "How did it make you feel," and onto, "Why did it make you feel that way," is a nice transition without a continuous "Why, why, why" approach.

"What do you mean by X, Y, and Z?" is a nice open question that gives the other person a wide berth to expand on what they have said. It is also a pretty neutral way to get deeper and can be supplemented with more "what do you mean" type questions as the topic gets unpacked or broken down further. Asking someone to tell you more when they finish making a point or stop speaking is not a question. However, it aligns with the previously mentioned approach in a broader sense.

In a conversation where someone opens up to you about something personal or about an issue that they are facing, you can offer your help in question form. Often, we feel embarrassed to ask for help, so it is great to get an offer. Flip the tables around, and if you get asked if you need help, and you do, then take the person up on their offer.

Before moving on to the nuts and bolts of question asking, i.e., the techniques, here is a list of questions that you can ask to deepen the conversation:

- What book has influenced you the most?
- Who was your role model when you were a kid?
- Has any person had a major influence on your life?
- Have you ever experienced recurring dreams?
- Have you ever had your heart broken?
- What does success mean to you personally?

- What is your opinion on evolution?
- When was the last time that you cried?
- Do you ever feel lonely?

Lest we forget to be tactical and time our questions correctly. But you know that by now.

Chapter 6

Let's Talk Techniques

Before we get there, let's have some fun with some fun facts about talking:

- A 2007 study concluded that both men and women speak around 16,000 words a day (Hartston, 2017).
- Men interrupt women three times as often as women interrupt men (Hartston, 2017).
- The technical term for talking in one's sleep is somniloquy or somniloquence.
- The opposite of talking isn't listening. The opposite of talking is waiting (Lebowitz, n.d.).

- The technical term for a fear of public speaking is glossophobia.
- In 2005, Spanish researchers showed that rats can be trained to distinguish spoken Japanese from spoken Dutch (Hecht, 2005).
- In a speech made in 1961, John F. Kennedy was recorded as speaking at 327 words per minute, the fastest rate of public speaking in history (Hartson, 2017).
- According to research in 2013, people spend 60% of conversations talking about themselves (Ward, 2013).
- Based on the findings of a 2015 study, the average Briton spends five months of their life talking about the weather (Geddes, 2015).
- There is a town called Talking Rock in the US state of Georgia. The origins of the name are unclear. Sadly, the rock does not talk.

Well, there you have it, ten interesting tidbits to help you out of a conversational jam when the chatter dies off.

We All Love a Good Acronym

Imagine if we said global positioning system instead of GPS, or automatic teller machine instead of ATM. It seems like a bit of a mission to say the whole thing. In conversation terms, there are some acronyms that can help you with things to say when you are being stretched thin. The acronyms are not meant to be said out loud, but rather internally, to jog your memory and rescue the discussion.

SBR (Specific, Broad, and Related)

I actually prefer a different order, as in broad, related, and specific. It just seems to flow better that way in terms of small talk to deep talk. But, no matter, we will approach it the Nate Anglin way. It is not clear if it was Anglin who came up with the acronyms himself, but they do apply and are a great arrow to have in your quiver for a rainy day (nothing to do with talking about the weather). By the way, Anglin is an investor, CEO, and performance coach.

Specific

This might sound a bit odd, but within specific, you get broad... kind of. What I mean is that the circumstances can be broad, and the question asked can be specific. If you are at a conference making small talk, you can specifically ask about why the person is at the conference, what profession they are in, and whether they have heard of the guest speakers before. If you are at a barbecue and you don't know many people, you can ask the host if he or she barbecues often or what their favorite meat is. Specificity can be used in so many different scenarios, from chatting to a fellow parent while you wait for your child after school to a discussion at a book launch or birthday party, and so on.

Broad

Casting the net wide and asking questions like, "did you grow up in Dubai," or "did you enjoy playing sports at school," or the famous, "do you have children?" These questions can be answered, followed by, "and you?" Using questions like this is a good way to kick off a conversation where there is nothing that specifically ties the participants together. Having children is something that everyone has an opinion on, and from the broad question about whether someone has children, a wealth of conversion that swings back and forth can be established. If the person does not have children, you can ask if they have nieces or nephews, and generally, the question will be answered and then thrown back at you. Remember the funnel question section? If not, here is a reminder. The broad question about children can be funneled down to more specific questions (partially why I am not sold on the order of the acronym—enough on that, though).

Related

The third word in the acronym could be a subcategory of "broad," but that wouldn't make for a great acronym. As a possible scenario, you find yourself in a conversation about guitars. That is kind of specific but broadly related to guitars is anything to do with music, be it bands, genres, eras, musicians, concerts, music-influenced fashion or protests, or other instruments. In another hypothetical situation, you could be in a foreign city and ask someone if they like the city. Again, the relation is broad but can be narrowed down to culture, cuisine, population, history, transport systems, different areas, prominent statues, or museums.

HPM (History, Philosophy, and Metaphor)

This acronym doesn't even need an order, it works in any way, and when you are struggling in a discussion and remember HPM, you can mix up the order. Not mix up as in mix and muddle, just a changeup in order depending on the occasion.

History

This can mean your personal history specific to the situation. At a birthday party, you can talk about another birthday party that you remember and can ask the other person if they have any interesting stories about birthday parties that they have attended in the past. In a more general sense, you could ask where the person grew up, which opens doors to a back-and-forth conversation. It is also a topic that everyone can talk about, and for those that are still overcoming social anxiety, talking about a city or area, or house that they lived in is not about them personally. Listening to someone's history can guide the chat in a deeper direction because we all have stories about our past, whether funny, embarrassing, or serious. You could even talk about actual well-known historical events, with a question such as, "where were you when the twin towers fell?" or "what do you think of the moon landing?"

Philosophy

Not everyone wants to get deep about the world's most fundamental questions about why we are here, where we came from, and where we are going. In addition, you could get onto some shaky ground if you believe in evolution and the other participant does not. But philosophy could be your own philosophy relating to exercise, for example. You could ask if the other party enjoys any form of exercise, then offer your philosophy, which may be that three days of exercise followed by two days of rest is how you approach your workouts. There will be situations where philosophical chat about politics, education, racism, immigration, and other relevant issues will be appropriate. Actual historical philosophers may be interesting to talk about. Perhaps, you should research some theories from famous philosophers, such as Descartes, "I think therefore I am" (Miceli, 2018). You could offer up your interpretation—the most popular is that he means that you need your brain to exist—and ask what the other person thinks.

Metaphor

Not in the absolute classic sense, but in a "this place reminds me of…" or "that song sounds like…," or "what you said makes me think of…" sense. If you are chatting and the conversation falls silent, you could pick out something that is happening around you and link it to something you remember or something that it looks, sounds, smells, or tastes like. My personal feeling is that if the discussion is waning and metaphors are not cropping up just by the by, then searching with one indicates a clutching-at-straws stage. That is okay, though. You can't expect every single conversation to flow smoothly. But we have dealt with that.

EDR (Emotion, Detail, and Restatement)

You know the drill... doesn't have to be in order, but for the sake of the wonders of the acronym, we will address them in order.

Emotion

You can express an emotion, such as saying that you are excited to do the fun run as it is a charity event. So not only will you be promoting health and fitness, but you will be running for a good cause. You could also ask someone how they feel about, say, flying or a vacation that they are planning. If the conversation gets deeper, you can speak about emotions associated with a break-up or the loss of a loved one. In a business sense, you may want to know if the other person felt inspired by a presentation, and you can even frame it in a statement way, such as "it seems like you were inspired by..." Although it is technically a statement, you are basically asking a question. Remember, not too deep too quickly. Don't go from "did you enjoy that joke," to "how did you feel when your father died."

Detail

This does depend on the type of conversation. Even if you are asking someone how their day was, which can be mundane, you can press for more detail and get the conversation moving. The same applies to asking someone about their hobby. As I have mentioned previously, it is easy to talk about a subject that you know a lot about, and people tend to know quite a bit about the activities that they enjoy. The "who, what, where, when, and why" questions can be of use as they promote sharing more detail, but again, don't press too hard if you sense a reluctance to talk further on a specific subject.

Restatement

Clarifying questions would fall under this category, and you would look to say that you understood what the other person said in whatever way. Then, you can ask if you were correct in your understanding. If you were, great, you can move on. But perhaps it is actually better not to have got it completely right because that way, the conversation has to flow—something to think about. If the chat is after an event, you can lead with a summary of what happened. Say at a sports fixture, and then compare opinions with the other person. This one can be a little difficult if the small talk is very generic, but you'll get there, don't worry.

That's it for the acronyms, and now onto a social interaction element that can prove awkward for both parties involved… but not after you've read this next section.

Compliments

Receiving a compliment can be awkward. Those of us who don't like the limelight will cringe at the thought of receiving a compliment in front of other people. However, some people will jump at the chance to be publicly complimented. The trick is just to take the compliment—say thank you and smile. Definitely easier said than done, my friends. If you are giving the compliment, you want it to come across in a way that is natural. You might face a situation where your compliment is 100% from the heart, but you struggle to get it across in a way that is sincere. This can happen when you are part of a discussion and you have your compliment ready, but are stressing so much about when to give the compliment, that you garble it and come across poorly. Let us prevent that.

Remember the section on body language? Specifically, the part about microexpressions that are instantaneous and involuntary. Well, if a compliment suddenly surfaces and the time is right, then pay the compliment immediately. If you like someone's shirt, you will realize that from the first time you see them, and if you tell them that you like their shirt, then a comfortable atmosphere should result. Hopefully, that person will take the compliment well. When receiving a compliment, humility is often observed, but also remember that playing down whatever it is that you have been complimented about can be taken as a lack of appreciation for the compliment.

Also, don't sit at home for hours trying to think of compliments. A natural element must remain, although a bit of preparation for possible compliments is encouraged. If you are going on a second date and a few traits from the first date impressed you, then you can come up with three things that you would like to compliment your potential suitor on. No need to use all three, but if you have options, there is less pressure. Here are some compliment tips to get you on your way:

- Be authentic in the way you speak and in your body language.
- If the compliment is meant to be specific, don't generalize it.
- Complimenting someone on doing well at something that they are passionate about will give that person a great feeling, even if it is awkward... but when doing so, remember bullet point one.
- Pay attention to things that the person has said, so you have a frame of reference to ask if they have done this or accomplished that, and from that point, you can issue the compliment.
- Avoid backhanded compliments. They usually involve a "but." For example, "you are a great singer, but..." Usually, good things are not preceded by "but."
- Compliment someone on something that *they* are proud of. A person accomplishing a goal of swimming a mile may not mean much to you, but you can still give the compliment. Achieving goals is deserving of compliments, for sure!

As the compliment recipient, you don't want to gloat or boast, but you could reply with a (genuine) compliment. Avoid going on a tangent about everything in your life that led up to your achievement. Be grateful, don't dwell, and let the discussion continue.

Bookmarking

I also like to call this signposting; a method of marking parts of the conversation that can lead to a deeper connection with the intention of returning to them. There are people that are natural bookmarkers and make their marks without any thought, and there are people that need to work at it. Let's break this down further.

Future Mentions

If someone mentions during a conversation that they like a particular restaurant, you can tell them that you also like it (make sure you like it) and that it could be fun to meet there for a meal. You have just placed a mark/put in a sign leading to a future meeting.

Inside Jokes

On occasion, something funny will happen which can be bookmarked as a recurring inside joke, that can be an icebreaker used more than once. It could be anything from spilling your coffee while talking to someone at a business breakfast to spilling your beer on someone in a pub. Those people might be unknown to you, but if you see them again, then you have an immediate way to start a chat, after the exchange of pleasantries.

Same Same

It so often happens that you meet someone that lived one street down or went to the same college or used to go to a club that you were always at. The "same, same" moment is the one where you realize something like the above. You have a subject in common to talk about, and you could bookmark it by saying that you will add that person on Facebook or Instagram and that you can then make an arrangement to meet up—bookmark inserted.

You Have to See…

…this movie, or read this article, or follow that person on Instagram. The next time you meet, you can flick to the bookmark and ask if they have seen, read, or followed, and a conversation can ensue without any awkwardness.

Chunking

We have to remember all sorts of things, like phone numbers, pins, passwords etc. Have you ever noticed that credit card numbers or phone numbers are separated, as in 084 7879 287. This number is separated into three parts comprising three numbers then four numbers then three numbers. The groupings of numbers have been chunked together, making the full number easier to recall. Unlike if it was written like this: 0847879287.

Chunking, in terms of talking, works in a similar way. You need to separate information so as not to overload the other person. This would be the case in an explanation situation. Let's assume someone is explaining how electricity works to you, and we'll assume you know very little. The person explaining is not going to throw the entirety of the information out at once. Instead, they will break the information into smaller chunks, separated by pauses.

It is believed that our brains can remember only seven bits of information at once, meaning that chunking is an essential skill when teaching people things, or explaining a concept. Logically, you need to use your chunks in order. This is not restricted to teaching or explaining, it could be a story about yourself. If you just go, go, go and throw everything out at once, the other person will get lost and confused, from which point it can be difficult to come back.

Saying No

Imagine if a friend asks you to go to the beach and you just don't feel like going. There is no reason, it is one of those times where you would rather stay home. It should be easy to say no, considering that you are friends. So many people, however, will say yes to keep their friend happy, which is the classic case of what we should not be doing. It is difficult to disappoint someone, especially someone we are close to, but we need to try and be true to ourselves. It would be different if your friend called you and said that they had just been broken up with. Being the shoulder to cry on is your duty as a friend, but you get what I'm saying.

There is a method called "yes, no, yes," and it is an effective way to deliver a positive no. The first yes is saying yes to yourself, as in choosing what *you* want to do, but internally. The beach example doesn't work for this one, so let's change that to a work situation. Your manager gives you a task, but you are so busy with your other work that you will only have time to do it in a few days when you have completed everything else. Many of us would just accept to keep the manager happy, but then it would take a long time to get the task done, and your manager will not be pleased at how long it took. Your *yes* in this case would be the yes to your decision, in this case to say that you can't, or at least can't do the task immediately. Next, comes your out loud *no*— politely but firmly and positively. Then, you put forward a suggestion that you can do it in a few days, or that you would be prepared to split duties with a colleague. Doing this is the second *yes*, and it kind of softens the blow of the no. In a workplace situation it shows conviction and conveys that you are prepared to work something out. Your manager or colleagues will appreciate your efforts.

Ending a Conversation

Everyone, and I mean *everyone,* has been in a conversation that they want to get out of. It doesn't mean that it is a bad conversation. If you have a valid reason because you are going to be late for something if you don't exit, then there is nothing rude about excusing yourself. I understand the anxiety that can rise as you think about your next engagement, while you are finding a spot to jump in and say, "not to be rude, but I have a meeting in 30 minutes and I am going to be late if I don't get going"—perfect exit.

In other situations, you might want to exit a conversation because you are bored or do not like the topic, which can be a little harder than leaving because of time constraints. There are some steps you can put in place to make conversation leaving a little bit easier.

Practice Your Exit Lines

It becomes slightly more straightforward if you know what you are going to say, as opposed to figuring out what you want to say and *when* to say it. Here are some examples:

- It was good to see you. Listen, I don't want to keep you, I'll find you on Facebook and we can connect at a later stage—very polite, and not dishonest.
- Work circumstances are easier, as you can excuse yourself mid-conversation by telling the other person that you need to get back to your tasks. In this setting, you can pick up the conversation at a later stage. Again, polite, and not dishonest.
- If you are at a party, you can say that you

need to ask the host something. You may actually just need a short break, so you go to the host, ask them your question and return to the conversation (if you want to).

- You could catch the eye of a friend and call them over to introduce them to the person you are talking to. After the introduction, you can say something like, "okay, I'll leave you two to chat." Let's just hope that you are not throwing your friend to the lions of a terrible conversation, but at the end of the day, the method works.

- Bringing the conversation back to the starting point brings a loop to a close, which can be used as an opportunity to exit. Obviously, you need to tactfully complete the loop before you excuse yourself.

Basically, you just have to be polite, as honest as possible, and get your timing on point. Try not to give negative signs such as fidgeting or looking at your watch, even though you will probably want to. If you fidget or look at your watch, the other person will pick up that body language and things could get awkward. The more you step out of your introverted comfort zone, the better you will get at leaving conversations.

When you leave a conversation, you may take with you a great story, so let's get to the skills needed to tell a good tale.

Chapter 7

How to Tell Stories That Stick

To tell a story, you need somewhat of an attention span, as you do to listen to a story. Our attention spans are reducing severely due to the immediacy of life. You can get any information almost instantly, plus social media fires quick information at us before we carry on scrolling. Before we get our storytelling hands dirty, I want to improve your knowledge of attention spans.

- The average human attention span is 8.25 seconds. This is less than a goldfish.
- Attention spans can range from 2 seconds to over 20 minutes.

- The average human attention span decreased by almost 25% from 2000 to 2015.
- When we don't get enough sleep, our brains don't have enough time to complete these important tasks.
- An individual's attention span varies depending on their age, with younger people usually having longer attention spans.
- Women usually have longer attention spans than men.
- Your attention span can also be affected by how emotionally engaged you're in a task.
- 1 in 4 teens forget important information about their close family and friends.
- Almost 1 in 10 people forget their own birthday from time to time.
- Almost 40% of Americans have forgotten one simple piece of information, and some have even lost one item they use on a daily basis in the last week.
- Attention span can be improved through various methods, such as mindfulness and meditation.

- The average person spends 2.7 minutes watching a video on the internet.
- The average audience attention span is only 8 to 10 minutes, which means you should keep your speeches short and engaging to hold your audience's attention.
- Paying attention is a key skill for learning, but children with autism (Schiller, 2023).

I am sure you are surprised at some of those stats, and are maybe questioning how the human race operates. Me too! But it doesn't matter, on we go.

The Science of Storytelling

Time to take a deep dive into your brain. After all, that is where the science is. Everyone is aware of the fight-or-flight scenario, where the brain chemicals are activated in such a way as to immediately prepare us by producing adrenaline and other chemicals. By telling a story well, we can evoke... well, get the other person or people to evoke the release of the right chemicals.

Dopamine

This chemical is associated with behavior that produces a high. Exercise and chocolate are two opposing dopamine triggers. So is sexual intercourse, and drugs. Try to avoid the drugs, and the gambling, which is another dopamine producer. That is how addictions work; hits of dopamine that last for shorter time spans. Conversations can be dopamine effective, especially if a story is being told to a group. The exerting parts of the story, the twists and turns, leaving the listeners wanting more, accompanied by good body language will encapsulate the group in a dopamine rush. A positive result among many is the enhancement of the focus of your audience. Another positive is that there are increased chances of listeners remembering your story. It will thus be most beneficial to get that dopamine flowing early on in the story, to hook your audience in.

Cortisol

Put simply, cortisol is the warning hormone, and in an engaging conversation, it pricks up its ears and concludes that there is something to be learned. This increases focus, and is most effective when triggered by danger or potentially intense parts of a story.

Sometimes, if you drop a horrendous and shocking fact, the cortisol can be produced in excess, causing discomfort and often anxiety. This is not to say that every person will produce cortisol. If you find the subject totally boring, then something shocking may not really be shocking for you.

Oxytocin

When mothers deliver babies, there is a rush of oxytocin, which develops the strongest bond that exists in human life. A baby is unbelievably vulnerable and needs that deeply strong bond. Logically, showing your vulnerabilities while talking to a group, kicks off empathy in your audience, and causes them to appreciate you more. Exposing vulnerabilities is damn difficult, especially for introverts, but you need listeners as much as you need storytellers. Whichever one you lean towards is absolutely fine... and hey, you might become both if you are not already.

Endorphins

Endorphins make you happy, and are stoked by lighthearted or funny moments. A connection is created, even in cases where the subject is a serious one, but where there is still room for a funny quip or two. You can link part of your story to a funny incident, and using a small tangent you can take the listeners to a humorous place and then return them to the seriousness.

All Together Now

It does take some skill. However, if you can create a story incorporating what needs to be said to get all four chemicals flowing, you will have your audience in a good place and the discussion or story will be an absolute success. To get some tips and examples, you can watch Ted Talks or formal debates on YouTube. Otherwise, you can go to talks on subjects you may like. Whichever you choose, remember that the exercise is observational, for future implementation. Pay attention and perhaps jot down some notes. This comes recommended.

The Elements of a Good Story

If you thought there were only four based on the brain chemicals, you would be wrong. There are many elements that act as contributors to the contents of the four categories. It is like having four umbrellas, under which there are other elements. Let's examine them.

Give a Preview

Remember back in the day when you went to see

a movie and there were trailers for other movies before the one you are there to watch starts? Of course, you do. The trailer is a preview that may or may not pique interest in the soon-to-be-released movie. We are working under the assumption that you are telling a story to a group, which means it will have some structure. Just like a movie trailer, you can incorporate small parts of the story in an effort to hook your audience and keep them interested via the promise of future entertainment.

The Cliffhanger

You want your audience to be present, both physically and mentally, so if you sow seeds of curiosity, and as the saying goes, keep them on the edge of their seats, you should be able to hold their attention as you build the story from the ground up.

The Element of Surprise

Saying something unexpected or rounding a point off with a sub-story that works as a surprise will hopefully endear the audience to you. Introducing an event, like the time you tried to rescue that elderly man from drowning, but were not successful. I don't know if that happened to you, but if it didn't then use another surprising sub-story that you were involved in.

Mystery

Saying something like, "I was at the beach, and there was a man who got washed out to see. I'll come back to that because it is quite interesting." You have just created mystery, which can work in conjunction with the cliffhanger element, leaving you wanting more. Creating mystery is also an audience-retention tactic, and is commonly known as one that garners good results.

Humor

As discussed above, a joke gets the endorphins flowing, which create happiness and/or joy. If we are feeling good as an audience member, we are likely to stay tuned, so to speak.

Wonder

Anecdotes or actual statistics can create a sense of wonder. Think back to the facts at the beginning of this chapter, and the facts throughout this book. Some are fascinating, almost unbelievable, and using any alarming or outrageous facts can have very good effects on a conversation.

Personal

Details about yourself that the audience can relate to, creates a personal atmosphere. In addition, information about anything that your listeners identify with is going to create a connection. It is easier if you are addressing a group about something relevant to you, but also to the group, then it is easier to get that connection going.

Drama

Draw it out tactfully, speak with expression and enthusiasm, or with emotion in your voice to get that soap-opera-type drama going. Okay, not quite that cheesy, but a watered down and more realistic version of dramatic storytelling.

Techniques for Delivery of the Story

We now know the elements that you want to incorporate into your story. Don't be fixated on incorporating every element. It is about context, but now we are going to delve deeper into the mechanisms of delivering your story.

Immerse Your Audience

If you are standing on a stage and your audience is some distance back, it is going to be difficult to connect—not impossible—just difficult. Hand gestures along with scanning your eyes across the room, so that you look at everyone in the room. When you lock eyes with audience members you naturally draw them in. Even though the listeners don't play a part in your story, you want to make them feel like they do. If you can spark imagination in a way that the audience is so immersed that they are activating their collective mind's eye, then you are doing a great job.

Tell a Personal Story

Hypothetically, you are gay, and struggled for years to come out of the closet. You were scared of judgment and homophobia. Perhaps, you felt that there was something wrong with you, and your parents would be embarrassed. After many years, you plucked up the courage to come out, and it was a liberating move, as you felt no judgment, but only love and support. You would have definitely gone through the emotional wringer, and telling your story in more detail than the hypothetical situation, will do wonders to hold the audience's attention. In telling a personal story, you garner empathy, which is an endearing emotion that attaches the speaker and the listeners emotionally.

Focus on the Characters in the Story

Whether you are telling a factual or fictional story, there will be characters. At the very least, there will be one character, probably yourself. But in your story, there will be parts about people that you came across, and again, you want to get the mind's eye activated. You need to be detailed in your descriptions, but not overly so.

- Too much detail
- John was just over six foot. His hair was thin, and would blow back and forth in the wind. John had brown eyes, and a crooked nose. You see, he broke it playing football. His chin was very pronounced and he had thick hair sprouting from his ears. The little blood vessels in his face had long since burst. Probably because of too much time in the sun and too much drinking over the years. John's neck was thick... etc. etc. etc.
- Right amount of detail
- John was tall with wavy hair. A distinctive feature was his crooked nose, and split blood vessels from sun exposure and excessive drinking.

You need to give the audience two or three

mental images of a character and they will fill in the gaps. Less is more in these cases.

Something Memorable

This could come anywhere in the story, and is something that you want your listeners to talk about later when they are at home. I heard a speech where the speaker was addressing PTSD and suicide. He incorporated a story about an 18-year-old who went to World War II, came back in his early twenties, and drank heavily until he reached his 60s. Through alcoholics anonymous, he got sober, but could not drown out his pain and his demons any more. He tried to commit suicide by drinking paint and trying to decapitate himself with a chainsaw. That story got some very loud "oooh's and ahhhh's." I will never forget that day, and the details of the talk as a whole. A quick word of advice is to make sure the memorable part is related to what you are talking about.

A Positive Ending

I will take the PTSD scenario. A positive ending could be something inspirational such as telling the audience that there is help for PTSD sufferers and individuals that have mental health issues. In this case, you would want to get the message out that things such as the near-suicide can be prevented by proper care. You don't want to go as far as your quintessential Hollywood happy ending, but an audience that leaves on a positive note, having been influenced by your other hash's techniques, will remember you, and talk about your story to others. In this PTSD case, your aim in addressing an audience would be to spread awareness and find ways to help. For that reason, it is good for the listeners to talk to others.

Some Quickfire Tips

Below are some extra tips on how to create a captivating story:

- A story, even if in anecdote form, has to build a scene.
- select a meaningful story
- have an idea of structure and develop the story as you go
- be clear on conveying what has changed near the end
- Practice. Especially if it is a speech at an event. Even introverts have to make speeches—you can't turn your brother or your best friend down, so don't think that you will exist for 60, 70, 80 years without having to address at least one audience.

Humor

I'm pretty sure that most people like to laugh, and you know the endorphin-creating aspect of humor. Not everyone can make the majority of a room laugh, but if you can develop the ability to create humor, it is another victory for compelling storytelling. You can introduce humor by borrowing elements of funny stories you have heard from friends or read in a book. Telling a joke in the classic sense of working up to a punchline is kind of outdated. The reason for that is that so often it comes across as cheesy, and pre-planned (not that planning is a bad thing). It might be too mechanical, so my advice is to go with a story and not a joke in the classic sense. Here are a few things to keep in mind when aiming at a humorous story or two:

- identify things that make you laugh
- identify things you already do that make others laugh
- use anecdotes
- learn the basics of humor
- don't be afraid of some self-deprecating humor

- keep working at it

You need to consider your audience and read the room. Perhaps, you have a story planned as part of a presentation, and while you are speaking, you realize from the crowd's reactions that the story will not be appropriate. The best solution is to abandon the story, and hopefully call on another story that you have as a backup. Making tiny mistakes, and fumbling every now and then will show the listeners your human side. Don't do it on purpose, but if it happens you can make a quick joke about it, and the crowd will forgive you. Consider why you want to tell a story. It may be for personal gain or to show off, in which cases you may want to reconsider telling it.

Taking tips from general observations, either in real life when you are out and about, or from live talks and content from television, books, or social media. Here are some more things you can try if you want to work on your humor:

- work on your observation skills
- study funny people
- learn how to read a room
- build a joke off of common ground

- give the opposite answer to yes/no questions
- play with numbers
- use a character switch
- make a running joke out of something
- make fun of yourself (but be gentle)
- know when to draw the line
- don't try too hard

The time has come to get a bit more generally specific. You will see what I mean.

Chapter 8

Simple Tips for Every Situation

"Conversation should touch everything, but should concentrate itself on nothing." –Oscar Wilde

O scar Wilde was a somewhat eccentric, part-prophetic poet and author from Ireland. Wilde lived in a simpler word, from 1854 to 1900, and the above quote illustrates how conversation should flow naturally between topics. It also indicates that a conversation should not be restricted by a plan that is not malleable, or by a plan at all. We could pick holes in the quote, but I am going to rather let you appreciate the romanticism in it. Well done, Oscar.

Let's start off with some conversation starting

questions, comments, and statements, broken down into different contextual situations.

Corporate Events

- This is my first time at this event. Have you been here before?
- What do you think of the food?
- I like the choice of theme for this event. What do you think?
- What's your favorite holiday?
- What do you enjoy most about events like these? (Herrity, 2022).

Conferences

- Will you come back to this conference next year?
- What's changed since you started attending this conference?
- What is the most important thing you learned since coming to this event?
- Which of the speakers has been most enjoyable for you so far?

- Will you be at the [panel/speaker name] session? I'm trying to decide whether to attend (Herrity, 2022).

Networking Events

- How many times have you attended this event?
- Hi, can I borrow your pen?
- I've been looking forward to this event for weeks!
- Do you sing? I noticed you have a deep voice.
- Hi, are you a [name of a profession]? (Herrity, 2022).

Casual Events

- How is your day/night going?
- What book has had the biggest effect on your career?
- How have your goals changed over the years?
- What do you hope to achieve in your professional life?

- What is your most outrageous professional goal? (Herrity, 2022).

Conversations Between Employees

- How long have you been working at this organization?
- Do you have any tips for working here?
- How would you rate your experience here so far?
- Where are the best lunch spots around here?
- Where are you planning to have your next vacation? (Herrity, 2022).

Getting Deep

- What career-related issues keep you up at night?
- Who is the most influential person in your professional life?
- Do you consider yourself a risk-taker? What is the biggest risk you've taken to advance your career?
- What is your idea of a perfect role?

- If you could go back in time, what would you change about your profession? (Herrity, 2022).

At the Start of an Interview

- It's a pleasure to meet you. How has your day been?
- What a nice place you have here.
- What do you like most about this company?
- How did your company achieve [insert success story] last year?
- I can see you're a fan of [mention their team]. Did you watch their last game? (Herrity, 2022).

A bit of an information overload, but you are not expected to memorize every question for every possible situation.

Networking

You may have heard of Business Network International (BNI). If not, it involves breakfast once a week at a restaurant. People from different professions attend. There may be a lawyer, a plumber, a caterer, an accountant etc., and the idea is that you refer business to each other. Everyone has a chance to speak about their profession, and then, breakfast, where networking and eating happens.

It is quite nerve-racking, but think back to the section about getting out of your comfort zone. A networking breakfast will definitely put you out of your comfort zone, but after you've struggled through it a few times, it will become easier and more enjoyable.

Joining a running club or a tennis club, if you like sports, is a chance to network. Not in a formal way like BNI, but a lot of networking happens casually in sports club environments.

Networking can actually take place anywhere. It doesn't have to be restricted to an official event. Asking people what they do for work is part of making small talk, and you can bet your bottom dollar that people pick up work in a variety of settings. With that in mind, it's time to look at some "across the board" networking advice, including formally arranged events and casual ones too.

You need to have a plan, and a fair amount of your plan is politeness. Before you will be seeing people that you have met once or twice, make a list of their names and anything specific that you noticed about them. In a formal sense, you should be able to jot down what they do for a living and perhaps a personal characteristic. If it is something very informal, like a kid's birthday party where you will be seeing other parents, you could write down the names, followed by a part of a discussion that you had at the last birthday party. It is worth mentioning that networking can be about many things, from getting participants for a survey to making friends after moving cities. Here are some proven ways of improving your networking abilities:

- Smile. Even if a stranger smiles at us, we tend to smile back, and we all know that when someone laughs in a group, that laugh can be contagious, even though you may not know what they are laughing at. When you meet people, look them in the eyes while you shake their hand and put a friendly smile on your face. A warm and welcoming demeanor does what those two words mean, making someone feel welcome in your warmth, which is hopefully mutual.

- Don't spend too much time on the small talk. If you can get the conversation to progress relatively rapidly to something more interesting than traffic, weather, or how nice the surroundings are, you will start to find out things about each other that are more fun or serious (in a good way) to talk about than the traffic jams the other day.

- Ask for opinions or suggestions. If you have been thinking about something, perhaps something as innocuous as what movie you would pick if faced with two choices, then use that to create conversation. For example, "have you seen Shawshank Redemption? I have been trying to figure out if I like Boondock Saints more. What do you think?" Use your imagination and get creative.

- Use your online presence. In a business sense, your company probably has a website and a social media presence. In a casual sense, you probably have a social media presence. In both scenarios, you can direct someone who you are chatting with to your social media. Don't be too forceful. Just throw it out there, and carry on as guided by the reaction. A quick tip within the tip: don't have a social media presence that is offensive, rude, or provocative.

- Keep your word. If you tell someone you will make contact with them, then stick to the arrangement. Whether you both enjoy tennis and you say that you will get hold of the other person to arrange a game—follow through. So often, we frivolously say things that we do not intend to do. Stop doing that!

- Always try to increase your social circle. You never know when you might need help, a friend, or someone to build you a wood-fired pizza oven.

- Occasion appropriateness. At a conference or networking event where there is a formal atmosphere… and… a buffet table, don't spend all your time at that table. I am quite aware that some of these events are wonderfully catered, but it will look like you are only there for the culinary experience. There will probably

be quite a lot of chit-chat based around
the food at a team-building barbeque, so
go ahead and eat while you network.

The Elevator Pitch

It is not done in an elevator but is named *the elevator pitch* because it is a summary of yourself that takes about the same time as you may spend in an elevator with a stranger. If you develop a pitch, you can confidently respond to the "tell me a bit about yourself" line, which we hear so often. The BNI example of having a short time to pitch your business is a good illustration of a pitch. Although probably longer than an elevator pitch, the pitch part of the pitch is still there. At the risk of repetition, I must emphasize that we are not looking at one type of event or occasion—your elevator pitch can, and hopefully will, be used in most situations where meeting people is involved. Here is what you need to do to become a good elevator pitcher:

- The first and most obvious requirement is to be brief. There is nothing worse than asking someone about themselves, and the next half an hour is spent listening to something that could have been said in a few minutes.

- In a formal networking environment, you need to be persuasive, and in a social sense, you need to be confident. I know it can be awkward talking about ourselves, but it is inevitable.

- Mention your goals. Let's say you are into fitness, and you mention that you do quite a bit of running. It would be a conversation-enhancing move to say that your goal is to do a half-marathon. It is likely that running is a big part of your identity and is something that could prompt the other party to talk about their fitness goals or other goals that they have in relation to a hobby or interest.

- Be positive. It isn't great listening to someone complain or be negative in general, and it isn't great being the complainer from a networking point of view. Yes, topics that attach to negativity will come up but don't dwell on them for too long.

Please don't forget that even though it is called

the elevator pitch, we are hoping that it will lead to a longer and more in-depth conversation. Make sure you have more to say than just the contents of your pitch.

Remembering Names

People have varying opinions on remembering, or should I say, forgetting names. Some don't think it is rude to forget a name, and then apologize, while asking for the name again. I agree with that opinion, and if I am the person whose name has been forgotten, I don't take offense. Considering this, you should make a concerted effort, and here is how you can improve your name-recalling skills:

- This is easiest to illustrate in a hypothetical conversation:
- Jack: "Hello, my name is Jack."
- Jill: "Jack, nice to meet you, Jack."
- Then quickly in your head (if you're Jill) you repeat "Jack" three times.
- Try to focus your thoughts on the introduction, instead of the next thing that you want to say.

- Often, you will be introduced to multiple people at once, in which case, remembering every name can be challenging... but, we must challenge ourselves.
- Connect the name with something. Maybe a facial feature or even another person with the same name, so if you need a memory jog you can think of the other person.
- When the conversation ends and you say goodbye, use the person's name, and when you get home, go over the names of people that you met.

Time for Romance

First dates can be daunting, and there will always be some nerves or anxiety. Running out of conversation can get the awkward thermometer skyrocketing, but there are some measures you can put in place to keep that thermometer on the low end.

Showing Interest

Not the hardest one... here is what to do:

- eye contact: window to the soul and all of that
- Keep your confidence up without being overbearing.
- Make sure your compliments are genuine.
- find some common ground; a hobby or interest
- If you feel that there is a lack of interest from the other party's side, your feeling will probably be correct, so back off and show them respect by doing so.

Asking

If you meet someone at a party and would like to see them again, all you need to do is ask if they would like to meet. Not that easy, I know, but you can apply the following:

- be assertive
- don't use the word date. Rather ask if they would like to meet for X, Y, or Z. Putting a label on it very early on also puts some pressure on it.
- once a connection is established, you have an "in." Don't wait too long to ask.

- Be yourself!

Questions on the "Date"

You can call it a date privately, but the first one is just two people meeting for conversation. Here are some good questions to ask:

- What are your passions?
- Tell me more about them, please.
- What do you do for work?
- Did you grow up here?
- What music/movies/food do you like?

Basically, slightly small talk focused but with serious potential to get deeper.

Date Ideas

Personal preference comes into play here, but the good old coffee date is a great place to start. Of course, you can throw out a few options, like a walk, a trip to an art gallery, a hike, a city bus tour, or anything else that has the potential to be fun. Your goal is to make a good impression, no matter what the activity is. Don't be fake or carry yourself in the way that you expect the other person to want. Being yourself is imperative—you want the person to like you for who you are.

Rejection

As I said in Chapter 1, not every person hits it off with every other person. Rejection is a bit of a negative word, but all it means is being turned down. You simply have to deal with it immediately by concluding that you and the other person are not going to work as a couple. It's not you. I promise.

Hopefully, you get the second date, and more thereafter

Conflict in Conversations

Discussions can turn into full-blow arguments, and the trigger of the conflict can be anything that you disagree on. Thing is that we don't have to agree on everything, but we can still have a productive and respectful conversation. That should be the goal, but conflict will arise at times. First, here are some unhealthy ways to handle conflict:

- not being able to identify or refusing to identify the other person's needs
- getting angry, belligerent, insulting, and nasty

- withdrawing and isolating the other person
- refusal to compromise or empathize
- avoiding conflict due to a fear of an adverse outcome

If there are unhealthy ways, then there must be healthy ways, which are as follows:

- showing empathy and preparedness to consider someone else's point of view
- speaking in a calm manner and showing respect
- the ability to forgive and forget
- be open to compromise
- accepting that facing conflict is the best option for everyone involved

On the very last point of facing conflict, nature provides us with a very good example. When a storm is approaching, cows will move away from the storm in an effort to avoid it. However, the storm always catches up with them, and they face the full brunt of it. Buffalos, on the other hand, head straight towards the storm, face its might, and after it passes, they find calm. The simple message that this metaphor gives is that facing conflict head-on is far better than running from it.

Awkward Conversations

They happen... every day, all around the world, but the whole chat may not be awkward, just a few moments worthy of cringing. Whichever way it goes, you can incorporate some of the following ways to deal with the awkwardness.

- Don't try to ignore it.
- Make a joke about it. Even if it is super cheesy, it will relieve some, hopefully, of the awkwardness.
- Avoid judgment.
- Don't try to fill the silence.
- Let it go.

Remember that the awkward conversation or moment is not going to hang around all the time. In addition, by this stage, I am super confident that you are well on your way to the goal of being able to carry a conversation with anyone!

Afterword

You made it! Well done!

There are a few things I would like to remind you of, starting with the fact it is okay to be nervous when you begin applying what you have learned. If you just stroll into conversations without any butter-flies, then you are probably not taking those conversations seriously.

Our comfort zones are so named because we feel comfortable within their boundaries. You are going to have to step outside those zones, and in doing so, you will grow as a conversationalist and as a person. You need to work towards a position where you look forward to social interactions, and not dread them. That brings me to time, and I would like to refer back to my explanation of having to be bad at something before you become good at it. Always remember that, especially when a conversation doesn't go well. It happens, don't cast self-judgment, learn from the experience and move forward.

I have mentioned the next point a few times, but it bears repeating. The world is not a place where everyone gets on with everyone. Some people click, others don't, and it is neither person's fault. If you can acknowledge that, then you are cutting yourself some slack, knowing that you won't always have amazing conversations. Look at it like a sport—some days a player excels, some days they put in a poor performance. On the same tack, conversations will be excellent on certain occasions, and poor on others. Normal!

Preparation is an important factor, but don't overdo it and hence overthink it. Entering a conversation with ten pre-learned topics will see you thinking about what to say next, instead of listening to the other person. Practice is a good tactic, as I mentioned, and further, a role play exercise can be beneficial for actual conversations.

Active listening is a skill of note, and by mixing it with empathetic listening, you will be on the right track. You need to make the other person feel comfortable, by showing them that you have genuine interest in the conversation. If it becomes a two-way street, then the discussion can flow back and forth, as it is enjoyed by you and your chit-chat partner.

Don't forget the lessons on body language. Avoid being closed off, not making eye contact, or having a demeanor that indicates lack of interest. The handshake is important, and so is remembering the other person's name. You don't want to get onto controversial ground straight away, but do not completely dispel the possibility. A discussion on a point of controversy can be rewarding, deep, *and* respectful. The same goes for talking too much about yourself, jumping all over the place, or interrupting often.

On the latter point, there may be a need for interruption to exit a conversation. Politely stopping the other person and explaining that you have an appointment to get to, holds no negative connotations. In terms of exit plans, you have to be confident, and you have to have a few options. This is where the *positive no* can come in, where your personal feeling is a yes to whatever it is that *you* want, making "no" the answer to the question, followed by something like, "I will send you a Facebook friend request, and we can carry on our discussion sometime soon"—please follow through and send the friend request.

You may or may not want to be a storyteller, but if you do, then the science in Chapter 7 will be of great assistance. Creating warmth and comfort with your audience establishes a connection, and you can relax as you progress through the story. Take note of the expansion of conversations in differing circumstances, and let it guide you to a wide array of situations, from corporate, to casual, to networking, to dating.

It is a bit of a minefield out there, but you will be fine! I sincerely hope that you have enjoyed reading this book as much as I have enjoyed writing it. I also sincerely hope that you have found the information useful. If so, it would be great if you could give the book a review, so that it can help a greater number of people.

I will leave you with a quote from Michel de Montaign, the 16th century philosopher, and allow you to do with it what you will:

"The most fruitful and natural exercise for our minds is conversation."

Bibliography

Ackerman, C. (2018, July 9). *What is Self-Confidence?* (+9 Proven Ways to Increase It). https://positivepsychology.com/self-confidence/

Anderson, C. (2022, December 16). *How to Give a Sincere Compliment.* https://www.rd.com/list/how-to-compliment/

Anglin, N. (2020, June 16). *3 Simple Acronyms To Help You Become A Better Conversationalist.* https://nateanglin.medium.com/3-simple-acronyms-to-help-you-become-a-better-conversationalist-7f583fcabd2c

Apa.org. (2012, January 11). *Stress in America:* Our Health at Risk. https://www.apa.org/news/press/releases/stress/2011/final-2011.pdf

Azman. T. (2022, December 8). *How to Read People:* 7 Secrets Cues From Body Language Experts. https://blog.mindvalley.com/body-language/

Barnard, D. (2022, February 22). *Examples of Positive and Negative Body Language.* https://virtualspeech.com/blog/examples-positive-and-negative-body-language

Betterhelp.com. (2023, March 31). *22 Body Language and Communication.* https://www.betterhelp.com/advice/body-language/22-body-language-examples-and-what-they-show/

Biggs, C. (2019, May 3). *5 Secrets of People That Give the Best Compliments.* https://www.apartmenttherapy.com/how-to-give-the-best-compliments-260943

Bloomerang, (n.d.). *The Science of Storytelling:* How to Evoke Emotion and Get Your Audience to Give. https://

bloomerang.co/blog/the-science-of-storytelling-how-to-evoke-emotion-and-get-your-audience-to-give/

Blumberg, P. (2022, August 26). *The 20 best first date ideas, according to relationship experts.* https://www.today.com/life/relationships/first-date-ideas-rcna44970

Boone, A. (n.d.). *Two Types of Gestures:* Illustrators and Emblems. https://ethos3.com/two-types-of-gestures-illustrators-and-emblems/

Bowe, J. (2021, August 17). *People Who Are Good at Small Talk Always Avoid These 7 Mistakes, Says Public Speaking Expert.* https://www.cnbc.com/2021/08/17/avoid-these-mistakes-if-you-want-to-be-good-at-small-talk-says-public-speaking-expert.html

Brennan, D. (2021, August 25). *How to Be More Empathetic.* https://www.webmd.com/balance/features/how-to-be-more-empathetic

Bullock, D. & Sanchez, R. (2022, August 5). *The Secret Science Behind the Power of Small Talk.* https://www.fastcompany.com/90747480/the-secret-science-behind-the-power-of-small-talk

Businessballs.com (n.d.). *Mehrabian's Communication Theory:* Verbal, Non-Verbal, Body Language. https://www.businessballs.com/communication-skills/mehrabians-communication-theory-verbal-non-verbal-body-language/

Careers.umbc. (n.d.) *10 Tips for Effective Networking.* https://careers.umbc.edu/students/network/networking101/tips/

Carolinemaguireauthor.com. *Does Making New Friends Make You Anxious?* Here's How to Make Small Talk So It's A Little Easier for You (Or Your Child). https://carolinemaguireauthor.com/how-to-make-small-talk/

Casarella, J. (2022, August 28). *7 Tips for Living With Social*

Anxiety. https://www.webmd.com/anxiety-panic/tips-for-living-with-social-anxiety

Catahan, S. (2021, November 3). *13 Ways to Actually Build Confidence in Yourself, From Experts.* https://www.mindbodygreen.com/articles/how-to-build-confidence

Changingminds.org. (n.d.). *Haptic Communication.* https://changingminds.org/explanations/behaviors/body_language/haptic_touch.htm

Changingminds.org. (n.d.). *Open Body Language.* https://changingminds.org/techniques/body/open_body.htm

Chanteray, J. (n.d.). *How to keep the conversation flowing at a networking event.* https://www.thejoyofbusiness.co.uk/how/conversation-flowing-networking-event/

Cherry, K. (2022, November 9). *How to Improve Your Self-Control.* https://www.verywellmind.com/psychology-of-self-control-4177125

Cherry, K. (2022, November 7). *What is Self-Esteem?* Your Sense of Your Personal Worth or Value. https://www.verywellmind.com/what-is-self-esteem-2795868

Chibana, N. (n.d.). *7 Storytelling Techniques Used by the Most Inspiring TED Presenters.* https://visme.co/blog/7-storytelling-techniques-used-by-the-most-inspiring-ted-presenters/

Clifford, C. (2016, September 21). *11 Memory Hacks to Remember the Names of Everyone You Meet.* https://www.cnbc.com/2016/09/21/11-memory-hacks-to-remember-the-names-of-everyone-you-meet.html

Colin, C. & Baedeker, R. (2014, July 28). *How to Turn Small Talk into Smart Conversation.* https://ideas.ted.com/how-to-turn-small-talk-into-smart-conversation/

Cp-journal.com. (2012, March 7). A *Look at Pacifying Behaviors -* A Look at Uncomfortable People. https://www.cp-journal.

com/a-look-at-pacifying-behaviors-uncovering-uncomfort
able-people/

Craig, H. (2019, March 4). *10 Ways to Build Trust in a Relation-ship.* https://positivepsychology.com/build-trust/

Cuncic, A. (2022, November 9). *What is Active Listening?* *https://www.verywellmind.com/what-is-active-listening-3024343*

Davenport, B. (2022, September 1). *33 of the Best Small Talk Topics and Questions.* https://liveboldandbloom.com/09/self-improvement/small-talk-topics

Davila, J. (2016, June 17). *Stop Trying to Fix Things, Just Listen!* https://www.psychologytoday.com/us/blog/skills-healthy-relationships/201606/stop-trying-fix-things-just-listen

Deadwiler, A. (2021, August 29). How To Ask Someone Out: 8 Tips From Dating Experts. https://www.mindbodygreen. com/articles/how-to-ask-someone-out

Dean, G. (2020, September 8). *Scribbling Women:* Alice Duer Miller, Famous and Then Forgotten. https://blogs.library.jhu. edu/2020/09/scribbling-women-alice-duer-miller-famous-and-then-forgotten/

Doolen, D. (n.d.). *The Art of Small Talk:* Why Small Talk at Work Has Big Benefits. https://www.careercontessa.com/ advice/small-talk/#:~:text=The%20Science%20of% 20Small%20Talk%20%2B%20Why%20Small%20Talk% 20Matters,-Small%20talk%20is&text=It's%20a%20social% 20lubricant%20that,with%20a%20few%20brief%20interac tions.

Doyle, A. (2022, March 28). *Active Listening Definition, Skills and Examples.* https://www.thebalancemoney.com/active-listening-skills-with-examples-2059684

Doyle, A. (2022, August 4). *How to Create an Elevator Pitch* (With Examples). https://www.thebalancemoney.com/eleva

tor-speech-examples-and-writing-tips-2061976

Duckworth, A., Grant, H., Loew, B., Oettingen, G. & Gollwitzer, M. (2011). *Self-Regulation Strategies Improve Self-Discipline in Adolescents:* Benefits of Mental Contrasting and Implementation Intentions. https://www.tandfonline.com/doi/abs/10.1080/01443410.2010.506003

Ellis, R. (2022, September 3). *Introvert Personality.* https://www.webmd.com/balance/introvert-personality-overview

Forbes.com. (2022, July 1). *14 Steps to Take a Networking Pitch to The Next Level.* https://www.forbes.com/sites/forbescoachescouncil/2022/07/01/14-steps-to-take-a-networking-pitch-to-the-next-level/?sh=68b2ac8d1fd7

Geddes, L. (2015, December 17). *More than nine in 10 Brits have talked about the weather in the last six hours. But is this unusual – and if so, is it their culture or the climate that makes them so obsessed?* https://www.bbc.com/future/article/20151214-why-do-brits-talk-about-the-weather-so-much

Goodwall.io. (2022, June 3). *How to Be More Patient:* 25 Tips for Increasing Patience in All Parts of Life. https://www.goodwall.io/blog/how-to-be-more-patient/

Graciousquotes.com. (2022). *46 Best Roy T. Bennett Quotes.* https://graciousquotes.com/roy-t-bennett/

Gupta, S. (2023, February 16). *What's the Difference Between Hearing and Listening?* https://www.verywellmind.com/hearing-vs-listening-what-s-the-difference-5196734

Harris, T. (2017, April 20). *4 Types of Questions to Ask in a Conversation to Keep it Going.* https://www.theexceptionalskills.com/4-types-questions-ask-conversation-keep-going/

Harappa. (2020, September 15). *The Role of Gestures in Communication.* https://harappa.education/harappa-diaries/gestures-and-body-language-in-communication/

Hartston, W. (2017, March 7). *Top 10 Facts About Talking.*

https://www.express.co.uk/life-style/life/775964/top-10-facts-talking-national-conversations-week

Hatrabits.com. (n.d.). *Storytelling: 15 techniques to spice up your story.* https://hatrabbits.com/en/storytelling/

Hecht, J. (2015, January 9). *Rats Show off Language Skills.* https://www.newscientist.com/article/dn6856-rats-show-off-language-skills/

Heggli, O., Konvalinka, I., Cabral, J., Brattico, E., Kringelbach, M. & Vuust, P. (2020, April 27). *Transient brain networks underlying interpersonal strategies during synchronized action.* *https://academic.oup.com/scan/article/16/1-2/19/5825511*

Herrity, J. (2022, December 13). *11 Active Listening Skills to Practice (With Examples).* https://www.indeed.com/career-advice/career-development/active-listening-skills

Herrity, J. (2022, October 1). *150 Helpful Conversation Starters for Networking Professionals.* https://www.indeed.com/career-advice/career-development/work-conversation-starters#:~:text=Conversation%20starters%20for%20profes sional%20gatherings&text=What%20do%20you%20love% 20most,important%20skill%20in%20your%20profession%3F

Heshmet, S. (2017, March 25). *10 Strategies for Developing Self-Control.* https://www.psychologytoday.com/intl/blog/science-choice/201703/10-strategies-developing-self-control

HRnews.co.uk. (2022, April 20). *How to Cultivate Charisma as an Introvert.* https://hrnews.co.uk/how-to-cultivate-charisma-as-an-introvert/

Hu, E. & Nguyen, H. (2022, April 28). *How to tell a captivating story* — from a wedding toast to a job interview. https://www.npr.org/2022/04/26/1094947453/how-to-tell-a-good-story

Indeed.com. (2022, November 9). *How to End a Conversation (Including Tips and Examples).* https://ca.indeed.com/career-advice/career-development/how-to-end-conversation

Jenkins, J. (2014, September 26). *Chunking* - Grouping Information for Clear Communication. https://www.managingameri cans.com/BlogFeed/Communication-Skills/CHUNKING-Grouping-Information-for-Clear-Communication.htm

Johnson-Davies, D. (2006, August 30). *Obituary:* Naguib Mahfouz. https://www.theguardian.com/books/2006/aug/30/culture.obituaries

King, P. (2021, March 22). *Helpful Acronyms.* https://social-skills-coaching.captivate.fm/episode/helpful-acronyms

Knapp, M. L. & Hall, J. A. (2014). *Nonverbal Communication in Human Interaction.* https://www.scienceofpeople.com/mouth-body-language/#_ftn

Lebow, H. (2022, May 16). *45+ Deep Conversation Starters to Bond with Friends and Family.* https://psychcentral.com/health/deep-conversation-startersc

Lenhardt, K. (2019, August 21). *97 Interesting Body Language Facts.* https://www.factretriever.com/body-language-facts

Lenski, T. (2022). *How to Confront Someone Without Seeming Confrontational.* https://tammylenski.com/how-to-confront-someone-without-being-confrontational/

Lindberg, S. (2018, September 27). *What's the Difference Between Listening and Hearing?* https://www.healthline.com/health/hearing-vs-listening

Luminlearning.com. (n.d.). *The Three A's of Active Listening.* https://courses.lumenlearning.com/wm-publicspeak-ing/chapter/the-three-as-of
-active-listening/

MacCloud, C. (n.d.). *Thoughts on Storytelling in Social Situations.* https://www.succeedsocially.com/storytelling

Mann, M., Hosman, C., Schaalma, H. & de Vries, N. (2004, August 1). *Self-Esteem in a Broad-Spectrum for Mental Health Promotion.* https://academic.oup.com/her/article/19/

4/357/560320

Mass, S. (2022, July 21). *Follow-Up Questions:* The Key to Have Meaningful Conversations. https://thetrulycharming.com/follow-up-questions-meaningful-conversations/

Masterclass.com. (2021, June 7). *How to Read Body Language:* 10 Ways to Recognize Non-Verbal Cues. https://www.master class.com/articles/how-to-read-body-language#5Gq9iMtKo9DluxOYgoGh9q

McKay, B. & McKay, K. (2021, September 25). *The 3 Elements of Charisma:* Power. https://www.artofmanliness.com/people/social-skills/the-3-elements-of-charisma-power/

McKay, B. & McKay, K. (2021, November 28). *The 3 Elements of Charisma:* Presence. https://www.artofmanliness.com/people/social-skills/the-3-elements-of-charisma-presence/

McKay, B. & McKay, K. (2021, September 25). *The 3 Elements of Charisma:* Warmth. https://www.artofmanliness.com/people/social-skills/the-3-elements-of-charisma-warmth/

Mehrabian, A. (1971). *Silent Messages.* Belmont, California: Wadsworth Publishing Company, Inc.

Mercado, C. & Hibel, L. (2017, February 16). *I love you from the bottom of my hypothalamus: The role of stress physiology in romantic pair bond formation and maintenance.* https://www.ncbi.nlm.nih.gov/pmc/articles/PMC6135532/

Miceli, C. (2018, November 26). *I Think Therefore I Am:* Descartes on the Foundations of Knowledge. https://1000word philosophy.com/2018/11/26/descartes-i-think-therefore-i-am/

Mindmaven.com (n.d.). *5 Actionable Tips to Develop Empathy and Become a More Empathetic Person. https://mindmaven.com/blog/5-tips-to-become-more-empathetic/*

Mindtools.com (n.d.). *How to Make Small Talk.* https://www.mindtools.com/a5w6dor/how-to-make-small-talk

Mindtools.com (n.d.). *Making a Great First Impression.* https://www.mindtools.com/a391uhu/making-a-great-first-impression

Mindtools.com (n.d.). *Questioning Techniques.* https://www.mindtools.com/a2baqhc/questioning-techniques

Mindwise.org. (n.d.). *Five Signs You May Have Social Anxiety.* https://www.mindwise.org/blog/mental-health/five-signs-you-may-have-social-anxiety/

Navarro, J. & Karlins, M. (2015). What Everybody is Saying: An Ex-FBI Agent's Guide to Speed-Reading People. //www.scienceofpeople.com/mouth-body-language/#_ftn2

Ncbi.nlm.nih.gov. (Hasson, U et al, 2012). *Brain to Brain Coupling:* A Mechanism for Creating and Sharing a Social World. https://www.ncbi.nlm.nih.gov/pmc/articles/PMC3269540/

Nhs.uk. (n.d.). *Social Anxiety* (Social Phobia). https://www.nhs.uk/mental-health/conditions/social-anxiety/#:~:text=You%20may%20have%20social%20anxiety,eating%20with%20company%20and%20parties

Nichols, R. (1957) *Listening is a 10 Part Skill.* https://www.listen.org/Resources/Documents/Nichols10PartSkill.pdf

Njoku, C. (2019, May 25). *5 Tips for Approaching Someone You're Attracted to.* https://guardian.ng/life/5-tips-for-approaching-someone-youre-attracted-to/

Parade.com. (2022, September 30). *250 Good Conversation Starters for Any Social Situation.* https://parade.com/969981/parade/conversation-starters/

Parashar, V. (n.d.). *How to Add Humor to Your Speech.* https://www.region10.org/r10website/assets/File/How%20to%20add%20humor%20to%20your%20speech.pdf

Pease, A. (2017). *The Definitive Book of Body Language:* How to read others' attitudes by their gestures. https://www.science ofpeople.com/mouth-body-language/

Perera, K. (n.d.). *Self Confidence and Optimism.* https://more-self esteem.com/more-self-esteem/self-confidence-tips-2/self-confidence-and-optimism/

Perry, E. (2023, January 30). Learn how to ask good questions to keep the conversation going. https://www.betterup.com/blog/how-to-ask-good-questions

Psychologistworld.com. (n.d.). *Eye Reading* (Body Language). https://www.psychologistworld.com/body-language/eyes

Raeburn, A. (2021, December 20). *10 Places Where Eye Contact is Not Recommended.* https://www.thetravel.com/10-places-where-eye-contact-is-not-recommended-10-places-where-the-locals-are-friendly/

Sander, V. (2020, January 15). *125 Great Small Talk Questions* (For Every Occasion). https://socialself.com/blog/small-talk-questions/

Sander, V. (2022, June 20). *20 Tips to Ask Good Questions: Examples and Common Mistakes.* https://socialself.com/blog/ask-questions/

Sandygerber.com. (n.d.). *7 Hand Gesture Body Language Tips to Influence Communication.* https://sandygerber.com/7-hand-gesture-body-language-tips-to-influence-communication/

Schnitker, S. (2012, June 26). *An Examination of Patience and Well-Being.* https://www.tandfonline.com/doi/abs/10.1080/17439760.2012.697185

Scott, E. (2022, September 8). *Apologizing Sincerely and Effectively.* https://www.verywellmind.com/how-to-apologize-more-sincerely-3144467

Semin, G. (2015, March 3). *The Smell of a Handshake.* https://www.ncbi.nlm.nih.gov/pmc/articles/PMC4345820/

Shiller, J. (2023, March 31). *Average Human Attention Span by*

Age: 31 Statistics. https://www.thetreetop.com/statistics/aver
age-human-attention-span

Simonis, D. (2021, February 18). *5 Ways for Introverts to Turn Small Talk into Big Talk.* https://introvertdear.com/news/5-ways-to-turn-small-talk-into-deep-talk/

Sinusoid, D. (2021, September 2). *The Psychology of Confidence:* Where it Stems From. https://www.shortform.com/blog/psychology-of-confidence/

Skillsyouneed.com. (n.d.). *Empathetic Listening.* https://www.skillsyouneed.com/ips/empathic-listening.html

Smith, S. (2022, July 26). *Which Colour Makes You More Confident.* https://thecarousel.com/beauty-fashion/fashion/which-colour-makes-you-more-confident/

Soken-Huberty, E. (n.d.). *10 Reasons Why Listening is Important.* https://theimportantsite.com/10-reasons-why-listening-is-important/

Strong, R. (2022, January 19). *7 tips to strike up a conversation with someone you're attracted to* — no matter how nervous you feel. https://www.insider.com/guides/health/sex-relation
ships/how-to-start-a-conversation

Stanborough, R. (2020, December 22). *How to be Charismatic:* The Science and Strategies of Likability. https://www.health
line.com/health/how-to-be-charismatic

Starlawest.com. (2023). *What are Your Pacifying Behaviors?* https://starlawest.com/2023/01/what-are-your-pacifying-behaviors/

Studysmarter.co.uk. (n.d.). *Paralanguage.* https://www.studys
marter.co.uk/explanations/english/pragmatics/paralanguage/

Sukhman, R. (n.d.). *Empathetic Listening*: Definition, Examples, and Skills. https://www.berkeleywellbeing.com/empathic-listening.html

Taylor, P. (n.d.). *Body Language Mouth* (Complete Guide). https://bodylanguagematters.com/body-language-mouth/

Taylor, P. (n.d.). *Body Language of the Eyes* (Learn to Read Eye Movement). https://bodylanguagematters.com/body-language-eyes/

Taylor, P. (n.d.). *What is Open Body Language* (Posture). https://bodylanguagematters.com/what-is-open-body-language/

Teng, K. (2022, May 25). *How to Navigate Uncomfortable Situations and Keep Your Dignity* Intact. https://www.thevectorimpact.com/how-to-deal-with-uncomfortable-situations/

Toastmasters.org. (n.d.). *The Art of Small Talk.* https://www.toastmasters.org/magazine/articles/the-art-of-small-talk

Tskhay, K., Zhu, R., Zou, C. & Rule, N. (2018). *Charisma in Everyday Life:* Conceptualization and Validation of the General Charisma Inventory. https://psycnet.apa.org/record/2017-31803-001?doi=1

Tutorialspoint.com. (n.d.). *Body Language* - Eye Movements. https://www.tutorialspoint.com/body_language/body_language_eye_movements.htm#:~:text=Looking%20to%20the%20right%20and,imagination%20and%20left%20activates%20memory.&text=When%20speaking%2C%20this%20could%20mean,being%20honest%20in%20his%20speech.

Ury, W. (n.d.) *The Power of a Positive No.* https://www.leadership-tools.com/a-positive-no.html

Van Edwards, V. (n.d.). 13 First Date Questions Backed by Science. https://www.scienceofpeople.com/first-date-questions/

Van Edwards, V. (n.d.). *How to Have and Hold Dazzling Conversation with Anyone:* We Review 11 Science Backed Steps. https://www.scienceofpeople.com/have-hold-conversation/

Van Edwards, V. (n.d.). *How to Network:* 18 Easy Networking Tips You Can Use Today. https://www.scienceofpeople.

com/networking/

Van Edwards, V. (n.d.). *How to Read People and Decode 7 Body Language Cues.* https://www.scienceofpeople.com/how-to-read-people/

Van Edwards, V. (n.d.). *How to Read People's Eye Direction and Behavior with 34 Clues.* https://www.scienceofpeople.com/read-people-eyes/

Van Edwards, V. (n.d.). *39 Mouth Body Language Gestures to Spot in Your Next Convo.* https://www.scienceofpeople.com/mouth-body-language/

Versace, A. (2022, July 3). *The Science of Small Talk - Why* Small Talk Has a Big Impact. https://www.thehrdigest.com/the-science-of-small-talk-why-small-talk-has-big-impact/

Wachter, H. (2018, December 19). *7 Ways to Become Trustworthy.* https://experiencelife.lifetime.life/article/7-ways-to-become-trustworthy/

Ward, A. (2013, July 16). The Neuroscience of Everybody's Favorite Topic. https://www.scientificamerican.com/article/the-neuroscience-of-everybody-favorite-topic-themselves/

Warrell, M. (2015, February 26). *Use it or Lose it:* The Science Behind Self-confidence. https://www.forbes.com/sites/margiewarrell/2015/02/26/build-self-confidence-5strategies/?sh=71275f3b6ade

Watkins, N. (2022, January 5). *How to Give Sincere Compliments.* https://socialself.com/blog/give-compliments/

Waters, S. (2022, January 12). *Understanding the Difference Between Sympathy and Empathy.* https://www.betterup.com/blog/empathy-vs-sympathy#:~:text=This%20means%20that%20both%20empathy,but%20from%20your%20own%20perspective.

Westsidetoastmasters.com. (n.d.). *The Eyes Have It.* https://westsidetoastmasters.com/resources/book_of_body_language/

chap8.html

Wooll, M. (2022, August 2). *Find Your Zen: 15* Tips on How to Be More Patient. https://www.betterup.com/blog/how-to-be-more-patient

Made in United States
Troutdale, OR
11/29/2023